DRY-FLY FISHING

DRY-FLY FISHING
Theory and Practice

F. M. HALFORD

with 26 plates

BARRY SHURLOCK

Barry Shurlock
& Co. (Publishers) Ltd
22 Gayhurst Close
Reading RG4 0QW

Introduction © David Jacques 1973
Reprinted from the first edition of 1889

ISBN 0 903330 02 4 *(standard edition)*
0 903330 03 2 *(de luxe edition)*

Originally dedicated to
GEORGE SELWYN MARRYAT
by his "grateful pupil"

Printed in Great Britain by
Redwood Press Limited
Trowbridge, Wiltshire

CONTENTS

LIST OF PLATES

INTRODUCTION

No assessment of Halford's contribution to fly fishing is valid if it fails to take into account the technology, the equipment and the mental attitudes prevalent at the waterside in the third quarter of the 19th century, when he cast his first fly. Fortunately, the years preceding and contemporary with Halford are revealed in a broad landscape through the writings of Bainbridge, Sir Humphry Davy, Lord Grey, Hofland, Kingsley, Ogden, Ronalds and many others, and it is to their contexture of events that we must turn for the fishing background that existed prior to the publication of Halford's volumes, the second of which is now re-issued. Even today, more than 80 years later, these writings provoke argument, not always dispassionate, wherever dry-fly fishing for trout has established itself.

Frederic Michael Halford was born in the year 1844 into a well-to-do family in the Midlands. At the age of 6, he caught his first fish, a 2 oz. perch, in a pond adjoining the garden of the house he lived in. Soon afterwards, the family moved to London, but the tiny perch had instilled in the boy an enthusiasm for fishing that grew with the years; and so at week-ends and during holidays he fished the Serpentine, and, as he grew older, the Thames for barbel, perch, pike, bream and trout, and the sea for whiting, cod, haddock and bass. He retained a love for coarse fishing that expressed itself in an article he wrote for *The Field* in 1891 under the name "Detached Badger", in the words "The bottom fishers are as true sportsmen as the most severe purists in fly fishing."

In 1868, after a brief period of salmon fishing, he was introduced to the Wandle, a pleasant stream running through the countryside south of London, and it was here that he cast his first fly. He was persuaded to fish the dry fly, for the simple reason that in the crystal clear water and in the narrow confines of the stream the wet-fly line, as it swung downstream, loomed conspicuously and menacingly over the trout and despatched them in panic to their holts in the weeds. Thus, at the very start his fly fishing was orientated in the direction of the dry fly, and to it he devoted the remainder of his leisure life.

His first fly rod was an 11', single-handed, 4-piece contraption with butt and joints of hickory and a top of whole cane. Many years later, in 1903, when describing it, he commented "the dry-fly fisherman of today would explode with laughter at the sight of this floppy, broken-backed implement . . ." Generally the rods used in his day were between 11' and 13', and about equally divided between single- and double-handed types. The blow line with its huge heavy rod was still in vogue, but its use was slowly diminishing. The materials from which rods were made were hickory, greenheart, whole cane and built cane, but it was soon realised that the heavier lines essential for casting into the wind were unsuitable for use with any but built cane. Ferrules were beginning to oust spliced joints, and were either screwed, tongued, suction, or of one of the many kinds' being pushed by ingenious inventors. The ferrules themselves were reinforced with bindings of wire or thread to prevent the joints coming adrift.

Lines were traditionally made of plaited silk and hair, but the hair broke and left sharp prickly bits protruding through the line surface, preventing it from running freely through the rod rings and twisting it into a horrible tangle. When fished dry, it became waterlogged, sagged and sank, and frequently broke the back of the weak rod when being lifted out of the water. Within months of Halford's introduction to the Wandle, the dressed silk line became available, and he at once recognised its superiority and adopted it. Reels were made of brass, and were of small diameter with a wide gap between the end plates. Heavy reels were preferred by many on the dubious grounds that their substantial weight stabilised the casting action and steadied the hand. Leaders were made up of gut, and flies were tied to gut.

Most of the Wandle members restricted their fly patterns to four types: Hare's Ear and Yellow for morning use; Red Quill for the afternoon and evening; East Wind when the wind was so blowing, and Hudson for use after dusk. That Halford followed the majority practice, and moreover brought many good trout to the net, will astonish readers to whom he was known (by reputation) as the apostle of scientific purism. Perhaps the memory of those days prompted the modest remark, ten years after the river Test had confuted his previous ideas and precipitated the research that led to his puristic reputation, that "there is too much presumption of superior scientific knowledge and skill on the part of the modern school of dry-fly fisherman . . ." (p.37).

It was in the year 1877, when Halford was in his early thirties, that he secured a rod on the Test as a member of the Houghton Club. To his consternation, he found it a different proposition to the Wandle, and its trout far more difficult to deceive. I cannot do better than to quote his own words.

My first visit [to the Test] showed me that this was quite a different class of fishing to any I had previously seen . . . . Until I made my first attempts on this historic Hampshire stream, I was really under the impression that I knew something of dry-fly fishing and fancied myself rather a good hand at it. I was quickly disillusioned . . . . the necessity for devoting myself to a prolonged study of the river, its fish and their habits, and the insects on which they fed, was soon strongly impressed on my mind.

(An Angler's Autobiography, p.76)

Halford discovered, as I and many others have since discovered, that although the odd fish on the Test can be induced by good presentation to take any artificial, imitative or not, the best chance of capturing a large

ix

wily one is with a fly that closely resembles the natural on the water or likely to be on the water at the time. This was nothing new; it was merely a return to the elementary principles of the ancients, but it required much study of the aquatic fauna of the river, a subject hardly known even to the most advanced anglers. Previous writers, including Alfred Ronalds, the most eminent so far, were vague and often incorrect. It comes as no surprise therefore to learn that before Halford's appearance on the literary scene the entomological knowledge of the Test fishermen was restricted to recognition of a mayfly, an alder and a "sedge", for no reliable manual existed that could provide a key to the flies an angler might encounter and upon which his quarry fed.

In those days, half the members fished the wet fly downstream, wielding heavy rods and blindly flailing the water with a pair of large flies attached to thick gut. Incredibly, minnow fishing was permitted in weir pools and hatch holes in May and August. But Halford's books caused a wind of change to blow through the water meadows, for gradually the wet-fly fishers, resentful of the innovating generation, resigned their memberships and were replaced by a younger group who leaned towards Halford's more delicate and selective art.

Halford has been described as the founder of the school of "exact imitation". This is odd, for I cannot for the life of me remember his use of the term. His language is tinged with moderation, as the reader will note (p.72) from his advocacy of "a fairly accurate imitation of the natural fly on the water", and again (Chapter VIII) from his refusal to believe that fish could discriminate between delicate gradations of colour, though colour could not be entirely disregarded. Indeed, his recognition of differences in the colour of natural insects of the same species and the same hatch is sufficient warranty that the term "exact imitation" would have been a solecism of particular absurdity to him.

The picture sometimes painted of Halford as a stern

unyielding ultra-purist will be rejected by readers of this volume. His philosophy of the dry fly was based solely on two postulates, the first that on certain rivers and in certain conditions it is the easiest way to catch trout, and the second that it is the most satisfying method of fishing known to mankind. It is true that his followers later stiffened his teachings into a rigid bigotry that permitted less variation in artifice than Nature allowed in her own work, but it was none of his doing. It is also true that in his later years he discarded many of his semi-generic flies and relied more on the imitative, probably because his greater skill in identifying insects made the former superfluous. The accusation that he disdained wet-fly fishers is repudiated in the second chapter of this book (p.37) and elsewhere by his expressed admiration of its practitioners.

That he made errors is not unexpected, but they are errors *de minimis*. The most valid criticism levelled against him is based on his opposition to the use of an artificial nymph for upstream casting to a rising fish. His reasoning was partly parochial and partly spurious; parochial because on the gnarled and knotted Test, its surface broken by twirls and tumbles, the surface film is almost non-existent, and thus no barrier prevents penetration by the hatching nymphs. In a flash they are through, and in a second or two have transformed into duns, and it is in this attire that they are known to the waiting trout. A hatching nymph would be an oddity to fish picking off winged flies. Spurious because Halford, on capturing a number of nymphs from the weeds and placing them in a tumbler of clear water noticed that every feeler or leg, and every fold or rib of their bodies was in continual motion. He refused to believe that trout could possibly mistake an artificial nymph, "that motionless, supine compound of dubbing, silk, quill and hackle" for the active ever-moving nymph.

Halford was obviously unaware that this activity was untypical, and due to agitation at the disturbance they had suffered. If he had followed a natural hatching nymph on its downstream journey, as I have done on the

Abbotts Barton stretch of the Itchen where Skues
developed his ideas, he would have noticed that its
struggles to penetrate the surface film were punctuated
with periods of rest while it drifted, helpless and
quiescent, an easy prey for the waiting trout, until it
gathered sufficient strength for another effort to break
through. It is during these resting periods that the
"motionless, supine compound of dubbing, silk, quill
and hackle" of the artificial can imitate the hatching
nymph splendidly.

When Halford cast his first artificial fly on the
Wandle, the natural insects of the trout's diet were
uncharted and unclassified, and hence the relationship
between them and their imitations left much to be
desired. This was not so important on relatively impov-
erished rivers, but on the rich chalk streams of southern
England where fly hatches were abundant and frequent,
artificials had to be reasonably close imitations of
current insects if they were to deceive the fish. It was
Halford's outstanding achievement that he completed
successfully the laborious task of classifying and describing the life histories of aquatic insects and relating
them to artificial flies; and although other aspects of
dry-fly fishing were surveyed in his writings, it is to his
peerless exposition of this relationship that the world of
fly fishing owes an everlasting tribute.

January 1973   DAVID JACQUES

DRY-FLY FISHING.

————•————

CHAPTER I.

THE DRY-FLY FISHERMAN'S GEAR.

BEFORE attempting to teach a novice how to fish with the floating fly, it may be desirable, as a preliminary step, to give some detailed information about the tools with which he is expected to work.

In this chapter it is my object to discuss calmly and without prejudice the pros and cons of each branch of the subject, in the hopes of inducing the rising generation of anglers to commence their study with the aid of the best devised and most suitable gear. Possibly I may in some instances even persuade experienced anglers to abandon what they have used for years, and substitute improvements which will tend to render the pursuit of their sport at once easier and more fascinating. One paramount difficulty occurs, and this is to avoid making one's self the means of puffing the wares of any one or more makers to the detriment of others who, although unknown to the author, may be as capable

of producing first-rate work, and as honest in supply-
ing it. If any names are mentioned here, it is only
because it is barely possible to describe the improvements made in various portions of the angler's gear
without in some instances referring to the names of
those who have made these particular improvements
their specialities. Although the word "dry" is used
as a qualifying adjective to the expression "fly fisherman" in the title of this chapter, it will, I hope, be
found that most, if not all, of the various kinds of
rods and tackle, as well as the reasons for and
against using them, will apply with as much force
to the votary of the sunk or wet-fly style as to the
most infatuated disciple of the floating fly.

The first and most important factor to be considered is the choice of a rod ; and on this question
the whole angling fraternity is divided into two totally
distinct schools, viz., those who advise the use of a
double-handed and those who prefer a single-handed
one for dry-fly fishing. The advocates of the double-
handed rod allege that with it they can throw a
longer line, and that at the same time the fly is
laid as lightly on the water as with the single-
handed. They also lay great stress on having more
power over a fish while playing it, and being better
able to keep a hooked trout from plunging headlong
into the nearest bed of weeds. On the other hand
the votaries of the single-handed rod deny that a
longer line can be thrown with a double-handed.
They also urge that any fancied advantage due to

greater power over the hooked fish is far more than outbalanced by the manifest disadvantage of having to carry and wield a heavier implement. Above all, they defend their preference on the ground of being able to cast with greater delicacy and accuracy, of being far less liable to break the fine gut in the act of striking, and in addition of being able to cast with greater ease against a much stronger adverse wind than is possible with the best balanced double-handed rod.

Personally I am, and have always been, entirely in accord with those who swear by the small single-handed rod, and have freely expressed this opinion at different times. Some friends have criticised and some utterly condemned this opinion. Those who have condemned it have quoted as a strong authority against me one of my best friends, now, alas! no more, the late Francis Francis. His name and his opinions have carried and ever must carry very great weight with all fly fishermen, whether they have known him personally or whether they have merely read his charming and ever fresh writings. He frequently discussed this question with Mr. Marryat and myself after a hard day's fishing together. On this one subject we never could agree; but at the same time Mr. Marryat and I, albeit strong advocates of our own idea, admitted freely that his contention might be right as to the two points of casting further through being able to hold up a much longer line, and not being so liable to catch the long grass behind the angler; and, in consequence of the greater power of the double-handed rod, having more command over a hooked fish. The late Mr. Francis, however, in that spirit of tolerance and justice which ever characterised him and endeared him to all who came in contact with him, conceded the point that for delicate or accurate casting *with* the wind, and in a far greater degree *against* the wind, the double-handed rod never had a chance with the single, and he himself in the last published edition of "A Book on Angling" (the sixth), inserted the following footnote on page 160: "I have seen 26 yards cast with a single-handed rod, and I also cast that length at the same time with the same line and rod. It was on the Old Barge river at Winchester that that was done, my friend Mr. Marryat being the other operator, and it was with his rod and line. I have heard of even longer casts than this."

This admission as to distance cast, coupled with the fact that he himself frequently carried a spare single-handed ten-foot rod for casting a comparatively short line to fish rising under his own bank, I think very much diminishes the strength of his own arguments. As I said before, however, we never could agree on this subject, and the conclusion of our argument invariably was the same, "Quot homines tot sententiae;" and on this angling subject alone we had to agree to differ.

Having determined to select a single-handed rod,

the points for consideration are, firstly, the material
from which the rod should be made; secondly, its
length; and thirdly, the style of action to be preferred. With regard to materials, it may be deemed
too positive an assertion to say so, but I think that
there are, practically speaking, only two open to the
would-be purchaser, namely, split cane, and greenheart. The greenheart is far less expensive, and
not much heavier than the glued-up split cane. It
certainly casts very well, and another very satisfactory feature about it is that it stands well after
continual whipping. Occasionally it has a knack of
breaking off short in a somewhat surprising way.

The fracture usually takes place in the lower or
stiffer portion of the rod. As an example, in a
three-joint rod it may be predicted that if this
accident happens it will be either just below or just
above the ferrule at the upper end of the butt.
Sometimes a flaw will be found in the timber to
account for it, and, with much of the cheap rubbish
sold to the unwary, another probable cause of fracture
at this part of the rod is the weakness produced by
ignorance, or possibly neglect, when boring the butt
to receive the tongue of the lower ferrule of the
middle joint, or what the rod-maker calls *the* joint.
This boring should never be carried as low as the
end of the female ferrule on the butt, otherwise a
weak place is invariably left. A very small practical
experiment in measuring will enable a purchaser
to make sure of this point when selecting his rod.

Very often, however, a greenheart rod broken in this way reflects no discredit whatever on the manufacturer. There is no flaw, the boring is not carried below the ferrule, and there is apparently no cause to account for the accident. In such a case it may be asserted that the angler himself is to blame.

He has smashed his rod by neglect of a primary desideratum for one who wishes to become a fisherman, namely, patience. He has returned his fly from the water and sent it swinging out behind him, but instead of waiting until his rod is released from the strain of this backward motion, has prematurely forced it forward again in the mistaken notion that this action will enable him to cast further. No timber can stand this double strain, and hence the smash. For all who only fish occasionally, and do not care to go to the expense of the glued cane rod, greenheart is pre-eminently *the* timber to select. It is not safe to buy even this at too low a price, as the timber should be thoroughly seasoned; the lengths intended to form each joint rent, not sawn; and the ferrules made of hard metal, properly fitted—all and each of which matters of detail add to the cost slightly, but far more to the efficiency of the rod.

For the fisherman for whom the comparatively small difference in price is not important, glued cane can be most strongly recommended. It is far superior in every way, and is well worth the difference in cost. It casts better and casts further,

and does the work with less labour both to the
angler and to the rod. In fact there is precisely
the same difference between a split cane and a greenheart rod as between a thoroughbred and an under-
bred horse. One answers when called upon for an
extra effort, the other shuts up. There seems to be
no limit to the responsive power of a first-class
glued-up cane rod in efficient hands, so long as the
line can be kept up off the ground behind the fisherman. In addition to this, the built cane rod will
slide four or five yards of slack line through the
rings when making a long cast, if a fairly heavy line
is used; to attempt this with a greenheart rod of
similar action would result in a broken rod.

When properly constructed the action of the built
cane rod is true; it bends equally from point to butt.
When returning, especially a very long line, it seems
to recover sooner from the forward strain of lifting
the line, and instead of quivering when the length
of line is behind the angler, seems to stiffen itself
at once, and hence to be sooner prepared to with-
stand the strain of the cast. Mathematically and
mechanically speaking, the hexagonal section is
the very strongest possible; and further than that,
in the method of manufacture all the outside bark,
which is the hardest, the most waterproof, and the
most elastic portion of the material, is used, while
the interior of the cane, which is soft, brittle, friable
sometimes, and worthless for purposes of rod-making,
is to a great degree discarded. Not many English

anglers will probably be inclined to make their own
rods ; but if they do, I can only advise them to read,
and read carefully, Mr. Henry P. Wells' book, entitled "Fly Rods and Fly Tackle," published a short
time since by Messrs. Sampson Low, Marston, Searle,
& Rivington. The author of this admirable work
has studied and carried out himself every part of
the process of rod-making in his own country, the
United States. He has probably seen much of the
American method of manufacture, and evidently he
is well able to appreciate the good and the bad
points of it. In fact, nearly all his advice is as good
as possible for the practical work of the rod-maker ;
excepting, perhaps, the question of ferrules, with
which I will deal later. It must, however, be remembered that to buy here or in America a glued
cane rod at a very low figure must of necessity cause
disappointment to the angler when he attempts
to use it. It is impossible to make a rod of this
description excepting at a comparatively high price.

Just consider successively the details of manufacture. First there is the cane. It has to be
selected, it has to be purchased, it has to be
seasoned, and seasoning is an operation which takes
very considerable time ; and on the question of
selection the judgment of a thoroughly experienced
workman and judge of this class of timber is
required—an experience which can only be got at
some cost. Having selected your cane, and having
seasoned it, the pieces fit for making the sections of

the rod have to be rent out of it (rent, not sawn).
Very many of the cheap and inferior rods sold here
are made of sawn sections; and it must be remembered that whereas the whole of the cane can be
sawn into the requisite pieces, comparatively only
a few sections fit for use can be split out of each
cane. These sections have then to be planed true
on two sides to an angle of 60 degrees. Six of
these sections have to be accurately fitted and
glued together to make each joint. They are
then securely bound with string and left until the
glue is set absolutely hard, and it takes many
months for the glue in the interior of the built
sections to set. When it is set the action of each
joint has to be tried, and the whole of the joints
making the rod have then to be put together
with temporary ferrules in order to judge what the
action of the entire rod will be.

Some of our friends may say that with a wooden
rod this same experiment has to be tried; but it
must be remembered that with the solid wood rod,
if it is too stiff, it is only necessary for the rod-
maker to mark the places where it is too stiff and
pare these portions of the joint or joints down.
But with the glued-up rod this is altogether impossible, because if he pares down the exterior of the
rod he will remove from it the bark, the only portion
which is of any value for rod-making; hence if
either of the joints be too stiff, it must be promptly
condemned as far as that particular rod is concerned.

Of course if it is too limber he has a chance, and his chance is to shorten this joint slightly; and if the result of this shortening is to render the joints of unequal length, the sale value of the rod is, owing to a somewhat absurd prejudice on the part of English sportsmen, much impaired. If any of my amateur friends should try making glued-up rods, they would probably be astonished to find how great an effect on the action of the rod is produced by cutting a very short piece off any one of the joints, and hence he can judge how easily, in attempting to remedy the above-mentioned fault, the rod can be made so stiff as to be utterly useless.

Having now tried the rod, and got the action of it quite true from end to end, and seen that the butt is strong and well set up; having also removed any superfluous glue from the surface, a considerable amount of time and labour has to be expended in whipping the rods with waxed silk at frequent intervals. On this point I do not agree with our American friends, who space their whippings much too far apart. Lately I have had all glued-up rods armed with whippings at intervals of about half an inch at the point to three-quarters of an inch at the butt; and this is to my mind a great improvement, as tending not only to increase the steely quality of the rod, but to save it from a probable smash when it is imperative to kill or cure by putting an undue strain on a hooked fish. Besides, it is an assistance to the rod on the occasions when an extra

long cast has to be made. It is an admirable plan
to whip greenheart rods in the same way, as it increases the stiffness but little and the spring very
considerably.

We now come to the question of varnish. Of
course the mere detail of laying on the varnish is
simple, and whether in England or in America work-
men who can accomplish it are easily found. The
English makers, however, are not as a rule so successful in the varnish they use as the Americans.
Some of the very best glued cane rods are made
in this country, and in all other respects they are
to my mind unmistakably better than the very
best of the Americans. After a season or so the
varnish usually cracks on the surface from the
mere action of the rod, damp gradually works under
the varnish, and it then peels off in flakes, exposing
the exterior portion of the cane (which perhaps is
not very important, as it is almost watertight), but
also exposing the glue in the joint, which in time
must suffer from the action of continual moisture.

In Mr. Wells' book full instructions are given on
every other detail of the manufacture of glued-up
rods, but strange to relate he is to a small degree
reticent as to the particular form of varnish used.
He calls it *coach body varnish*, and further on says,
"I use 'Valentine's Quick Levelling Varnish.'" I
am told that different carriage builders use different
varnishes for this purpose. I suspect that he means
copal, and this very likely is one of the best varnishes

to use for the purpose. If English rod-makers adopt it generally their customers must, however, give them a little more time to carry out repairs if they expect them to revarnish, as it takes several days to dry, and practically weeks to become adequately hard.

Some anglers prefer spliced to jointed rods, urging as their reason for this preference that the action of a spliced rod is more uniform throughout than that of an equally well-made rod in which the joints are connected by the usual metal ferrules. Before the use of thin hard metal for ferrules, when they were made of heavy soft brass tubing, there might have been some good grounds for this, but with the more modern form of metal ferrules the action with a properly balanced and thoroughly well-finished rod is uniform throughout.

Besides the trouble of splicing each time the rod is taken down, to my mind a great objection to the principle is that the splice is never thoroughly firm and sound unless the two taper ends of the joint are cemented or glued together, when the rod is practically in one piece. There is always more or less tendency in the splice to work looser and looser, and a very small degree of *give* in it utterly ruins the action of the rod. Mr. Wells has in his book, entitled " The American Salmon Fisherman," exhaustively argued out the mechanical and practical disadvantages of the splice, and to those who disagree with me I would commend the study of pages

33 to 37 in his valuable work. Having determined to use ferrules, I must confess myself unable
on this one particular point to agree with Mr.
Wells, who is a strong advocate for the simple
parallel fitting as against the ordinary tongued
ones used in this country. On this point I speak
with great diffidence, believing that he *may possibly*
be right, and that the unpleasant experience I have
had when using rods fitted with the simple ferrule
has been due to imperfections in the manufacture—
to imperfections of fitting accurately the male to
the female ferrule. But mechanically his argument
may be right. If both ferrules are perfectly circular in section and fit accurately the entire length,
there may be no tendency in one joint to become
separated from the other in the act of casting,
although such rods have not in my experience
been seen in this country.

Candidly, however, I doubt the correctness of his
theory mechanically. It seems that any action producing a tendency in the line to fly forward must
have a precisely similar effect on the fittings of the
joints by the friction of the line in the rings. This,
though slight at each cast, is evidently cumulative, and
must in time slacken, and if not remedied, sooner
or later propel the top joint from the ferrule. Until
some marked improvement is made in this point,
I must recommend our English anglers to select
the tongued ferrule, and invariably to tie the joints
together with the ordinary hitcher arrangement.

Neglect of this precaution is very likely to gradually work the top joint out of the fitting, until at last the entire strain is thrown on the tongue, which, being then loose in the socket, gets broken off.

If, however, they are willing to go to some little extra expense to save themselves this trouble of tying the joints together, they can do so by using a screw fitting made by Messrs. Hardy Brothers. There are other screw fittings made and illustrated in the Badminton series, but I have not found either of them satisfactory in use. If the male ferrules are smeared with old curd soap before putting the rod together, the joints will very seldom get jammed. If they should, however, get so firmly fixed that they cannot be easily taken apart, a few drops of paraffin placed on the top of the female ferrule will in a few minutes find its way into the fitting and remedy the fault.

The rod rings may be either upright, for those who prefer them (and of all upright forms that known as the *snake* is the best), or they may be of the ordinary loose pattern. The line passes a little more freely through the former, and the advantage of the latter is that when packed in the case there is less likelihood of their becoming broken or injured. In either case they should be made of hard German silver. The point ring should be of the Bickerdyke pattern, or what I think quite as good, a steel ring revolving in an eye made of the same wire as the rings. The winch fittings should be of the ordinary description, and nothing further would require to be said on this subject if tackle-makers had realised what other trades have been compelled to do, namely, the necessity of uniformity.   Every little maker, however, now-a-days thinks he has achieved some distinction in making the scoop of his winch either extraordinarily large or particularly small, so that the ordinary winch fitting as fixed on the rod in the one case will not admit of the reel being put in place, and in the other will not hold it steadily without the trouble of packing with paper or some such substance.   Hence, probably, Herr Emil Weeger's invention, adopted by Messrs. Hardy, of a conical fitting at the lower end to take the scoop, and a ring with very considerable range to secure the forward end of it.

Some makers and some anglers are very wroth at the idea of having a spear at the end of the rod. Its disadvantage is that when playing the fish it is uncomfortable, and if made too pointed or sharp may even injure the fisherman or his waterproof. But if it is made quite blunt and round at the end there is the immense advantage of being able to stand your rod up in the ground, so that there is no likelihood of its being trampled on either by yourself, your fellow-fisherman, or cattle on the meadow.   When spearing the rod, never jam it into the ground with a jerk, as this sets the ferrules tight, shakes the rod, and especially, if it happens

to strike a stone, is likely to break the winch.
Take the butt of the rod with both hands just
above the reel, and press the spear steadily into the
ground.

Now as to the length of the rod to be selected.
At the time when Mr. Francis published the first
edition of his book on Angling, dry-fly fishing was
comparatively unknown; and as the angler had only
occasionally to make a cast, and never to keep his
fly in the air while working backwards and forwards to dry it, the exertion of wielding a comparatively long rod was very slight. Hence we find
that of the four single-handed rods spoken of by
him the shortest was 11 ft. 7 in., and the longest
12 ft. 8 in.; and he himself says that a single-handed
rod " should not be less than 10 or more than 13 ft.
in length." I do not think that the argument that
men in those days were more muscular or more
hardy than we are at present is worth any serious
consideration; and hence I impute this advice to
the fact of the principles of dry-fly fishing being
then in their infancy. In the present day no trout-
fisher can require a rod anything longer than 11 ft.,
and from this to 9 ft. 6 in. are the dimensions every
practical rod-maker or angler would recommend.

With an eleven-foot rod past masters in the art
can cover a fish at from 26 to 30 yards, and with a
short rod of 9 ft. 6 in., one who knows how to use it
can put a fly in the teeth of anything short of a positive hurricane. In connection with this question of

length, further remarks as to the reel line must later on be considered. If the angler will not use the modern heavy class of line, he must, to make a long throw, have a somewhat longer rod.

The action of a rod must be absolutely true and even in every direction from point to handle. There must be no weak place in it, and at the same time no part which is unduly stiff. It should return quickly. The meaning of this is, that when trying the rods, by imitating the action of casting and forcing the point forwards, thus bending the rod, the point should recover and spring rapidly back to a straight line, and when there it should not vibrate, but quickly regain its point of rest, and remain rigid. This simply means that the elasticity of the whole rod is both uniform and smart, the material of which it is built thoroughly good, and the tapering proportionately carried throughout its length. For dry-fly fishing it certainly should of the two be rather stiff than limber; but at the same time it is not recommended to use a thing like a barge pole, which cannot by any possibility cast lightly or with ease.

American rods, judging from what one sees here, are too whippy for our insular ideas, and seem generally to lack backbone. They are also rather light in the point, the effect of which is to render it difficult if not impossible to recover a long line with them. The fashion of the present day is to use a rod that is slightly top heavy; and although this is

B

more trying to the wrist, yet, considering all points, it is a fault the right way.

There has been lately, in one section of the sporting press, some controversy as to who can claim to be the original inventor of the steel-centred rod. This may rouse the curiosity of readers; but if the point is considered as to the possibility of the invention being of any practical use to the angling world, the only conclusion to be arrived at probably is that it is waste of ink and paper. The idea is to build the sections of the cane on a central core of steel. I believe it is also suggested to treat the wood rods in the same way. Now the word *steel* suggests itself to the casual reader as giving the idea of just what should be in a rod. Mr. Wells in his book goes so far as to say that the rod of the future will be the steel one. That may be, but he is certainly too well versed in mechanics to suggest the union of two materials having such totally different action as steel and timber. One must naturally bend and naturally recover itself far more quickly than the other. For a moment consider the effect of rigidly fastening the two materials together. The one with the quicker action must of necessity tend to hurry the slower material, and the one with the slower action must equally of necessity tend to retard the action of the quicker material. What must be the effect? A tendency to disintegrate their union, and some considerable inconvenience to the hand attempting to use it. So far, my remarks on steel-centred rods have been based upon theory. As for practice, I cannot personally say much. I have handled experimentally some ten or twelve made by one of the best rod-makers in the United Kingdom. The price has in each case been considerably in excess of that of a glued cane rod, and my verdict has invariably been most unfavourable. They have not cast better; they have not cast more easily; they have not cast more accurately than the ordinary split cane by the same maker; they are certainly more tiring to the wrist, and when killing a fish I do not think that they have really given any accession of power.

As to reels, there is not much to be said. The old-fashioned one has been greatly improved by the more modern pattern with the handle on the revolving plate. There must be a check. Some anglers lay great stress on having a silent one, but, with no particular reason for it, I prefer the old-fashioned noisy one, which certainly gives forth to my ears agreeable music on the first rush of a three-pounder. There is, however, in connection with the check one point to which tacklemakers should pay a little more attention, and that is its strength, or in other words the resistance which it offers to the line being taken off it. As a rule it is far too strong, and hence even when striking from the reel (and no other style of striking can by any possibility be considered satisfactory), one does occasionally leave a fly in a fish which lighter action in the reel would have saved.

As the result of a rough-and-ready experiment, Mr.
Marryat is of opinion that when casting about 15
yards of the modern heavy line, if the hand is kept
off the reel line, at each cast or recovery of the rod
just one single click should be heard as the line is
drawn off. Of the size of the scoop I have already
spoken under "Rods," and only revert to the point to
urge on all successful tackle-makers in the United
Kingdom to do what the makers of microscopic ob-
jectives decided some years back, namely, to agree
among themselves as to one uniform length, thickness, and curve.

Reels are as a rule in this country either of brass
or of ebonite. The ebonite is far lighter, and as
one has to carry the weight all day long, this to
my mind is a very important factor. Some anglers
prefer a brass reel, and they urge that it is less liable
to be broken than one of so brittle a material as
ebonite. And here they are to a certain extent right,
although I find that a first-rate ebonite reel made of
the improved material now in use, treated with ordinary care, will last many seasons. There is another
argument used by both anglers and sometimes tackle-
makers in favour of the brass reel,—an argument
which to my mind is the most incomprehensible on
the part of the angler, and the most ignorant on the
part of the tackle-maker. It is that the heavy brass
reel at the butt end of the rod tends to balance it.
All that can be said is this, that if the rod-maker is
so totally ignorant of his own trade as not to be able

to make a rod fairly balanced without loading it with
a lump of metal at the butt end, which lump of
metal must throughout the day, when casting, inconvenience the wrist of the angler, it is time he was
taught better.   On the other hand, many first-rate
anglers differ with me on this point, and prefer the
heavy metal reel, thinking that it gives an impression of lightness in the point and steadiness in the
hand when casting.

We now come to the question of the line, and on
this question I would ask the reader's most careful
consideration, having devoted a very considerable
time to that branch of the subject. A reel-line
should be made of pure silk. This sounds like an
axiom, and it is one ; but unfortunately, in the present age, owing to the mania for extreme cheapness,
adulteration is so much the rule, that to find a pure
silk line is to-day not altogether an easy matter.
Then it should be plaited solid.

There are three methods of plaiting lines : plaiting them hollow ; plaiting on a core ; plaiting solid.
In the first they are worked on a wire, which is
withdrawn as the plaiting proceeds. If a piece is
cut off the end of a line made on this principle, it
can be detected with the naked eye, and the manufacturer, knowing this, has attempted to substitute the
second, a class of manufacture which produces a line
not to any great extent stronger than the first, but one
which will yet at a casual glance pass muster for a
solid line—that is to say, he takes a core of *silk* occa-

sionally, but far more often of *jute*, and on this core
he plaits a very thin tube of pure silk. This class
of line is most unreliable and in every way to be
avoided; and if only anglers would insist upon
having solid pure silk lines, one of their troubles,
especially when far from home, would be avoided.

Having, then, your silk line, it must be dressed or
waterproofed; and here again the manufacturer, in
his desire to produce a cheap article, and to produce it quickly, has gone out of his way to use a
most unsatisfactory class of preparation. He coats
it with some substance consisting chiefly of varnish,
or shellac, or gold size, any one of which is of
necessity brittle, and hence utterly unfit for the
purpose required. Then, again, he soaks the line
for a short time in this preparation, and it takes
up on the external surface a small quantity of this
brittle substance; the effect of which is that, as soon
as the dressing cracks, the water gets in and the
line very soon becomes utterly rotten. Such being
the case, some three years ago I consulted one of
the most practical tackle-makers with whom I have
ever been acquainted, one who understood his busi-
ness thoroughly and was willing to discuss, experiment, and improve any point brought to his notice.
This was the late Mr. Deller, of Messrs. Eaton &
Deller. He quite agreed with me as to the unsatisfactory nature of the line sold, and the first
hint he gave me was a most valuable one. He told
me that some years ago the lines were dressed

under the air-pump, and the moment he used that
word it was a revelation to me.   He further told
me that a certain number of lines had ever since
been dressed in this way, and that he was prepared
to try any necessary experiments on the subject.

After trying various substances for dressing, we
arrived at the conclusion that nothing but pure
boiled oil could be used; that by soaking the line
in the boiled oil under the air-pump, it could be
dressed perfectly throughout.   The effect of soaking
the lines in the boiled oil under the exhausted
receiver of the air-pump is to draw all the air *out*,
and thus force the oil *into* every interstice of the
line.   When our experiments had reached a certain
pitch, he made and sold a considerable number of
lines dressed in this way.   Unfortunately, to my great
regret, he died before the conclusion of our experiments.   He was pre-eminently one who believed in
the necessity of putting thoroughly good material and
thoroughly good work into everything he turned out.

After his death I consulted a very good friend,
Mr. Hawksley, an angler of some experience, who,
being thoroughly versed in practical mechanics, was
able within a very short time to effect considerable
improvements in the details of line-dressing; and
the lines that he has dressed are to my mind so
successful, so thoroughly smooth throughout, so perfectly waterproof, and at the same time so supple,
that I cannot help feeling that to the angler himself
or to the tackle-maker I shall be doing a consider-

able service in publishing in his own words the
exact process he uses. He says :—

" Immerse the line in a flat vessel containing pure
boiled oil ; place the vessel under the receiver of
an air-pump ; exhaust until all air-bubbles are
drawn to the surface ; do not remove the line until
all the bubbles have broken and vanished. Take
the line out of the oil ; draw it through your
fingers or a piece of flannel or felt lightly, so
as to remove all superfluous oil. Then wind the
line on a frame, as sketched on fig. 1. The

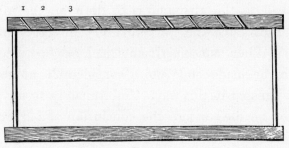

Fig. 1.

frame, which should be about 18 inches long, is
made of two side-pieces of wood, with two pieces of
iron wire across the ends. There are saw-gates cut
obliquely on one of the wooden sides of the frame.
One end of the line when covered with the first coat
of oil is fastened in the saw-gate marked No. 1, and
the line wound on. The frame and line is then
placed in an oven, heated to the temperature of 150°
Fahrenheit, and baked for about ten hours. The line
is taken out of the oven, and when cold, all irregularities rubbed off carefully with very fine glass-paper,

taking care not to abrade any of the silky fibres. After
all the irregularities are rubbed off and the line made
as equal in size as possible, it is again put into the oil,
under the air-pump, and the air again exhausted. The
line, when all the air-bubbles have broken, is taken
out, and again wound on the frame, being fastened at
the saw-gate No. 2, and so on; so that the line
should have a different point of contact with the
iron wire after each coat. The line on the frame is
again heated for about ten hours in the oven, repeat-
ing the operation as described ten times, rubbing
down after each coat is baked and cold. When the
fifth coat is reached, use finely-powdered pumice,
dry, on a piece of felt or flannel, instead of the glass-
paper used previously. The pumice powder will
leave a smooth dull surface. The last two coats will
not require to be rubbed down, and will give the
line a finished, glazed appearance."

A line dressed thus only requires to be thoroughly
rubbed over with red-deer fat, and the red-deer fat
to be occasionally renewed as the line is used, to
be, to my mind, as near perfect as possible.

Now as to substance of line. It must be fairly
heavy in the middle part; for a fairly stiff rod, as
heavy as shown on fig. 2. It must then taper to as

FIG. 2.

fine a point as the angler dare use. The length of
the taper is a very important point, and if I had to fix
upon an absolute one, I should say that from thickest

to finest it should be five yards long. However, Eaton & Deller invariably make the line with a six-yard taper, to allow a small amount to be cut off as it becomes weak from use. As a matter of economy, it is well to have a taper worked on either end of the line. When the tapered point has been too much reduced in length, the whole of the original taper should be cut off, and a new tapered point can be spliced to the central parallel portion of the line with waxed silk. It is impossible to cast against the wind with a light line, and it is even easier to cast down-wind with the heavy one than with the light. One of the reasons, perhaps, why glued cane rods cast into the wind better than wooden ones is that, other things being equal, they carry a heavier line.

Gut collars must be made of the very best gut procurable, and I am afraid it is not always easy to get it. Even a high price will not always command it, as some of the veriest rubbish ever produced has been offered to me at almost prohibitive figures. The knot to be used in attaching the collar to the reel-line is shown on fig. 3. The

FIG. 3.

length of the cast should vary from, say, three and

a half to as little as one and a half yards, the variation in length being necessary for variations in the
direction and strength of the wind. A convenient
plan, and one I adopt myself, is to knot up, say, two
yards of undrawn gut tapered from stout to as fine
as you can get, and also to keep a few fine-drawn
points made of three fairly long strands. A few
of these points and a few lengths of gut, and possibly a spare cast, should be kept in a wet box
between two layers of flannel, to enable the angler
to make his repairs on the spot; as, if a break takes
place, it is almost invariably in the fine point, which
is the weakest place, and with the wet box the
angler has always reserve gut soft and ready to tie.

A convenient and very portable form of wet box
has been brought out lately by Mr. Hawksley, and
is, I believe, kept in stock by G. Holland of Salis-
bury. It is illustrated on fig. 4. It is, however,

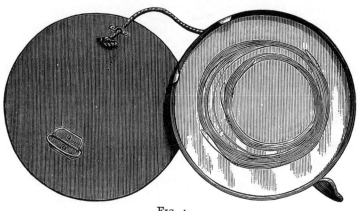

FIG. 4.

well to avoid leaving the gut too long in the wet

box, as in time it certainly rots it. After a fish has weeded, you should make it a rule to examine the gut; it will probably be frayed. If so, test its strength, and if necessary break off and tie on a fresh point. The gut should be soaked in lukewarm water until quite soft before attempting to tie the strands together; and of all knots for the purpose, I think that the double one illustrated on fig. 5 is the safest to use; although not quite so neat in appearance as a single one tied the same way, it is far more reliable. As to the colour of the gut, I do not like it too white, and, from the

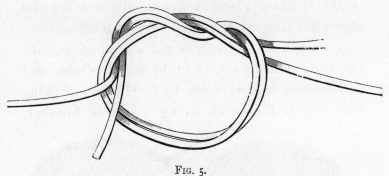

FIG. 5.

experience of all the streams I have fished, do not care about the colour that some tackle-makers affect, which I think must have been designed with the idea that the angler intended to pay a visit to the *Styx*. A slight blue-grey dye can be easily given to gut by immersing in a decoction of logwood with a very small portion of copperas; or it can be dyed in the " slate " dye made by Messrs. Crawshaw, illustrated in " Floating Flies and How

to Dress Them." It is said that the quality of the
gut is very much impaired by the bleaching treatment it meets with in Spain ; but I fear that anglers
have not sufficient influence with the trade to work
any special improvement on this point.

I have no intention of boring my readers with
much theorising on the subject of hooks, as it has
lately been ventilated both in the angling press and
in various books published on the subject. I have
in " Floating Flies and How to Dress Them " given
all the arguments I can advance in favour of the
use of eyed-hooks, and if I have not succeeded in
convincing my readers, I fear the case is hopeless.
Candidly, I can find no possible advantage in the use
of the old-fashioned hook whipped to a piece of gut.

Of course I cannot close my eyes to the fact that
a diversity of opinion prevails throughout the craft
as to the comparative merits of the turned-down
and the turned-up eye.   Mr. Cholmondeley-Pennell
has argued the point from his own particular
view, and has not altogether had the worst of the
argument. He asked me to give the turned-down
hooks a fair trial. Knowing that up to that time
I had been an advocate for the turned-up in preference to the turned-down eye, which he preferred, he
sent me a number of hooks selected by himself. He
asked me to dress my own patterns of flies on them,
and to try whether I should not arrive at the same
conclusion as he had himself, namely, that the turned-
down eye was less likely to miss a rising fish, and

more likely to hold him when once hooked, than the
turned-up. I tried these experiments as carefully as
I possibly could in the spring of 1886. I dressed
the same patterns on turned-up and turned-down
hooks. I placed them side by side in a box, and
when the fish were rising used them alternately.
The result was that I could find no difference
either in hooking or holding fish when hooked.
Both were as successful as usual and failed about
as often as usual; and I think that I may say, as
a simple fact, that where these hooks were used
alternately, they actually killed precisely the same
number of fish. I had, however, when dressing the
flies, one grave complaint to make respecting the
turned-down hooks, and that was the inferior manner in which they had been tempered. I think
I broke more than one-half of those sent to me.
This of course is not an argument against the shape
or form of the hook, but a strong condemnation of
the manner in which the details of manufacture were
carried out.

The original knot recommended by Mr. Hall for
attaching flies on eyed-hooks to the cast is illus-

FIG. 6.

trated on fig. 6; and Major Turle's knot, which is
certainly far easier to tie, and, practically speaking,

as secure when once tied, is shown on figs. 7, 8, 9,
10, and 11.

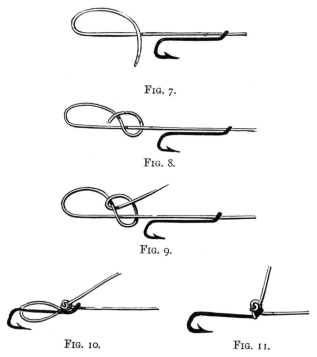

Fig. 7.

Fig. 8.

Fig. 9.

Fig. 10.   Fig. 11.

Where fish run anything like large, a landing-
net is a necessity. One with a solid ring, either
of wood, metal, or whalebone, with a handle long
enough to reach the fish in the water, and a turn-
over joint for the convenience of carrying, is to be
preferred. Every maker has his own particular
pattern, and many of them have points in their
favour. I think it is perhaps a convenience to
carry the net on a separate sling hung on the right
shoulder, so that it is under the left side. Of course
a basket or bag to contain the fish and tackle, &c.,

is a necessity. Bags are not so comfortable as baskets, and especially in wet weather are liable to strike damp and cold against the body of the angler carrying it. Fish also lose more in appearance when carried in a bag than in a basket, especially the under ones, if there are many. A basket which will make a seat is more cumbersome and less sightly, but altogether, I think, a convenience.

As to carrying flies, they may be packed in a book. I do not think, if carefully put away, the fact of flattening them is of much importance, as the first half-dozen whips through the air will, as a rule, restore them to their original shape; but for the angler who cares very much about the appearance of his flies when he first puts them on, perhaps a metal box in which the flies could be stood up, sticking into felt fastened to the bottom, is more convenient. A convenient form of box for the pocket with space for a pair of pliers is illustrated on fig. 12. A pair of scissors and a spring-balance for weighing the fish are almost necessities, and a loop of string at the end of the spring-balance, to be passed under the gills, will be found more convenient, and not disfigure the fish as much as the hook usually placed there.

As wading is often necessary, and persistency in attempting it without protection frequently leads in later middle life to rheumatism and other allied complaints, I am afraid that the inconvenience of *waders* must be borne. Stockings are lighter, but with them

of course one cannot go in so deep as with trousers.
In a gradually increasing depth of water, when nearly
up to the top of your wading stockings, it is a good

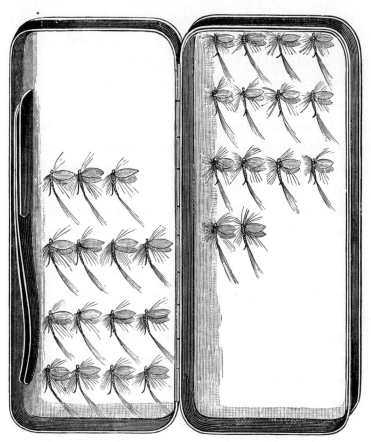

Fig. 12.

plan to hold up the inner edges with the fingers of
the left hand. The water-level will be felt on the
fingers, and often save the angler from wading too far.

When wading, it is best to take short steps,

c

planting the whole weight on the forward foot before advancing the other. The brogues should be fairly stout, and for wading on gravel should have nails in the soles, but for rock should have soles of felt. For fastening them, nothing is so comfortable as plain porpoise-hide laces, and nothing so objectionable as those straps and buckles which always sooner or later get out of order, and under which the line is liable to catch when fishing.

A short mackintosh must be carried in so variable a climate as this. A convenient method of carrying the waterproof is to fasten it on the top of the basket, folded a trifle longer than the breadth of the basket-lid. Straps may be used for this purpose, but two stout strings of about the substance of blind-cord are preferable to straps, as, after being thoroughly wetted, the string will get dry in time, and not remain sodden and messy, like leather. Besides, there are no buckles to come off and get lost, and if anything does go wrong with them, they can be repaired or replaced easily and anywhere. Each string should be passed through two openings in the lid of the creel, and have a loop at one end and a knot at the other. They are tied in a single bow, as shown on fig. 13, and one pull at the knotted end of each string releases the mackintosh. As far as dress is concerned, generally, woollen materials only should be worn. The form of costume should be such as to give the greatest possible freedom to the muscles, and the clothing should be made of a somewhat

light greyish or greenish neutral tint. When returning from a days fishing, every sensible man who
wishes to preserve his health should change every
particle of his clothing which is in the slightest

FIG. 13.

degree damp, whether from perspiration or rain, and,
if such a luxury is available, a warm bath before
changing will tend much to the comfort and enjoy-
ment of the evening meal.

CHAPTER II.

FLOATING FLIES AND SUNK FLIES.

THE simplest definition of the term "floating fly" is—
an artificial fly fished *on* the surface; and that of the
term " sunk fly "—one fished *below* the surface of the
water. To carry the definition a trifle further, a
floating fly, whether it is *cocked*, or, in other words,
floating with the wings up, or *flat*, that is, lying on its
side, is an imitation of a winged insect, either emerging or emerged from the nymph state, on the surface of the stream, while the sunk fly is an imitation
of the larva or nymph moving in the water, or of a
winged insect when water-logged or drowned. In
principle the two methods of fishing are totally and
entirely distinct. With the dry or floating fly the
angler has in the first instance to find a rising fish,
to note accurately the position of, or what is technically called *spot*, the rise, and to cast to this fish to
the exclusion of any chance work in other parts of
the stream. With the sunk or wet fly, on the other
hand, he casts to a likely place, whether he has or
has not seen a rise there (more frequently he has
not), and, in fact, his judgment should tend to tell
him where, from his knowledge of the habits of the

fish, they are most likely to be found in position or ready to feed. Thus wet-fly fishing is often termed "fishing the water," in contradistinction to the expression "fishing the rise," which is applied to the method of the dry-fly fisherman.

In treating of the advantages of dry-fly over wet-fly fishing, I am most desirous of avoiding any expression which should tend to depreciate in any way the skill exhibited by the experienced and intelligent followers of the wet fly. They require not only most undoubted judgment of the character of water frequented at various times of the day and season by feeding fish, not only a very full knowledge of the different species and genera of insects forming the food of the fish, not only a full perception of the advantages of fishing up-stream under one set of conditions and of fishing down-stream under others; but, in addition to all this, great skill in placing their flies accurately in the desired position, and allowing them to drift down in a natural manner and without any drag or check over the precise spot they wish to try. There is far too much presumption of superior scientific knowledge and skill on the part of the modern school of dry-fly fishermen, and I should be the last to wish to write a line tending to encourage this erroneous assumption of superiority, or to depreciate in any way the patience and perseverance, coupled with an intuitive perception of the habits of the fish, requisite for a really first-rate performer with the wet fly. The late

Francis Francis said that "the judicious and perfect application of dry, wet, and mid-water fly-fishing stamps the finished fly-fisher with the hall-mark of efficiency." This sentiment is to my mind pre-eminently characteristic of its author, and worthy of repetition by any of his admirers in later times.

Under certain circumstances the dry fly has in every stream great advantages over the wet, and in rivers where it is not generally used has the further advantage, that, from the fish being unaccustomed to see anything but the *natural* fly floating down cocked over them, they are altogether unsuspicious of the artificial, and take it with such confidence as to render their being hooked, if not their capture, almost a certainty. To define the circumstances specially suited to the dry fly is not difficult. When a fish is seen to be feeding on the surface, when the angler can ascertain the species of insect on which the fish is feeding, when he can imitate it, when he can present this imitation to the fish in its natural position and following precisely the course taken by the natural insect, and when he can carry out all these conditions at the first cast, so as to delude the fish before he has any suspicion of being fished for, the rising and hooking of the most wary trout or grayling is almost a foregone conclusion for the dry-fly fisherman.

It must be remembered that the only possible means of establishing a satisfactory connection between the fish and the fisherman is the medium of sight. A fish's sight is much more highly developed than any other sense, it being questionable whether he has any hearing, or whether his power of smell with surface food is sufficient to guide him in discriminating between the natural and artificial fly. Hence keeping out of sight is a most essential point to study; in fact, as before said, the fish should be hooked before he has any suspicion of being fished for. On the other hand, where no rising or bulging fish are to be seen, and whence it may be inferred that the fish are not taking surface food at all, the conditions are favourable for the use of the sunk fly. Even under these conditions it will sometimes occur that the floating fly is more efficacious than the wet.

Whatever advantages can be claimed for the sunk fly elsewhere, however, there are streams and conditions of weather in which it cannot be considered as having the smallest chance against the floating fly. As to conditions of weather, on the stillest days, with the hottest sun and in the clearest water, the fish are generally on the surface, when the wet-fly fisher would consider the conditions most unpropitious and unlikely. On such days to kill fish is most satisfactory and gratifying to the angler's bump of self-esteem, and often the largest and most suspicious fish feeding under such conditions seem quite guileless and fall victims to the art of the dry-fly fisherman, and nowhere so freely and so frequently as in rivers where the sunk fly only is habitually used. As to the streams in which the dry fly is under all circumstances likely to be more successful than the wet, those which rise from springs filtering up through a substratum of chalk or limestone, and in which the water is usually of the very clearest even after heavy rain, where the current is only moderately rapid, and which are usually in the summer months fully covered with weeds, and hence well stocked with larvæ of Ephemeridæ, Phryganidæ, and other water-bred insects, are pre-eminently fitted for the floating fly. These are usually styled "chalk streams," and it is said that there are days when even in the clearest of them the sunk fly is found more killing than the floating one. This may possibly be true, but in many years' experience such days have not fallen to my lot, and I should be inclined to consider them as *happening ones*, or, in other words, as the rare exceptions which go to prove the rule. Perhaps the best direct proof of this rule may be deduced from the fact that every Hampshire fisherman who has persistently studied the subject from season to season has gradually become more and more convinced of the necessity of imitating Nature as accurately as possible, and presenting the imitation in the most natural position, *i.e.*, floating and *cocked*.

In Derbyshire, a few years back, every one used two, and many three, four, or even more flies; every one fished down-stream, and fished the water. Now hosts of anglers have invaded the district, the trout and grayling are as shy and wary as any in the country, and what is the result? Day after day, and year after year, more of the successful anglers in the district fish up-stream with floating flies and over rising fish only, and it is only on an occasional blustering day that one of the old school succeeds in getting a moderate bag. The same tale can be told of all parts of the country, where the local anglers, taught from childhood to fish with sunk fly, laugh at the possibility of a bag being made with dry fly. As an example of this. Not many years ago, in Dorchester, one of the best dry-fly fisher-men of the day was seriously suspected, and even accused, of not fishing fair, because he succeeded in killing great numbers of the largest fish on days when the natives with wet fly could do no good at all. At length his proceedings were quietly but thoroughly watched by one of the local talent, with the result that he who went to discover a fraud found that he had been for years following a mis-taken policy, and went openly to his talented brother angler and told him all the circumstances, persuaded him to enrol him among his pupils, to teach him the art of dry-fly fishing, and at length himself became a votary of this style and a proficient in it, and ever after forswore the wet fly, and himself was able in turn to teach and convert others to the more modern and more successful school of angling. From north and south, from east and west, in later times fly-fisher-men came to Winchester, and when there, *saw, learned, and conquered* the use of the floating fly;

and although they could very likely only succeed in killing their two or three trout daily, yet very soon preferred them to heavier bags taken elsewhere with the sunk fly. They carried the information all over the country, until at length the spread of dry-fly fishing has become something dreadful to contemplate, because in the rivers where it is practised the fish never get a rest, but day after day, week after week, and month after month, are continually and continuously tempted to their destruction, or worse still, perhaps, rendered more wary, more shy, and more suspicious. It is even questionable whether the bad features of this spread of dry-fly fishing end here, and whether the perpetual danger of taking surface-food does not in time keep the fish down, and even make abstention from floating insects an hereditary instinct. This, too, is probably enhanced by the fact of the free-rising fish being gradually but surely killed off, and the new generations being bred from those who habitually find their food on the bottom of the river, so that each generation is less likely to rise than the one immediately preceding it. Possibly, too, the introduction of artificially fed trout into the rivers still further increases their tendency to prefer the comparatively safe shrimps, caddis, snails, and larvæ to the perilous experiment of taking surface food.

Some dry-fly fishermen are such purists that they will not under any circumstances whatever make a single cast except over rising fish, and prefer to

remain idle the entire day rather than attempt to
persuade the wary inhabitants of the stream to rise
at an artificial fly, unless they have previously seen
a natural one taken in the same position.   Although
respecting their scruples, this is, in my humble
opinion, riding the hobby to death, and I for one
am a strong advocate for floating a cocked fly over
a likely place, even if no movement of a feeding fish
has been seen there.   By a likely place, such a one
as a bare gravel patch between weeds on a shallow
is meant, or a point under the bank to which every
natural insect must be carried by the stream or
wind, on either of which there is almost invariably
a fish either feeding or ready to feed at the first
hatch of fly.   There is no doubt, too, that an angler
catching sight of a trout or grayling lying near the
surface or in position for feeding can often tempt
him with a good imitation of the fly on the water
floated accurately over him at the first cast.

Another great mistake often indulged in, even by
anglers of great experience, is to commiserate with
the votary of the dry fly in blustering or rainy
weather; and one's friends, when seeking to extenuate
one's want of sport, frequently express the opinion
that it was "too rough or too wet for the dry fly."
Why too rough or too wet ?   The natural duns bred
in the water are seldom if ever drowned in their
native element, however rough the weather may be.
At times the delicate Ephemeridæ are whirled over
and over by sudden gusts, but they still float, and,

as a matter of fact, a rough day with a good curling
ripple on the surface of the water is the day beyond
all others when the floating fly, if quite dry, cocked,
and accurately delivered, makes the greatest score,
and utterly defeats the sunk fly. The true difficulty
of a rough day is to spot the rise and place the fly
accurately, not to float it; and on a rainy day, although it is undoubtedly hard work to dry the fly,
yet, when once dried, it is undoubtedly far more
deadly than the wet fly.

We are often told that Mr. ——, the great Scotch
fly-fisher, is quite sure he can kill any number of
trout in a south-country stream, fishing in his own
style, and is prepared to make a match against the
best local man. Southron fly-fishers are not in the
habit of fishing matches and weighing in catches
at clubs, but occasionally one of these professors
is invited to try his infallible system on one of their
streams, and the invariable result is that, if he is
obstinate, and so firmly wedded to his opinions that
the stern logic of facts cannot move him, he returns
with the dictum that there are very few fish in the
river, or that the wind is wrong, or the water too
low, or some other plausible excuse. If, on the
other hand, he is a true lover of the art and not
above learning, he quickly discovers that his method
is not successful with the dainty over-fed fish of a
chalk-stream, and before long he becomes a convert
to the dry fly, and, I shrewdly suspect, uses it in hot
bright weather to advantage in his native brooks.

A dry-fly fisher must expect to miss an abnormally large proportion of rises, owing to the very small flies he uses, and some of our friends are apt to quote this as an argument against the Hampshire school, forgetting that even if an unduly large proportion are missed, yet in places, and on days hot, bright, and calm, when the sunk fly is utterly hopeless, the chalk-stream fisher will rise fish after fish, and his excitement will be kept up by hopes of success, from morning to night.   On one point all must agree, viz., that fishing up-stream with the finest of gut and floating the tiniest of flies, where every movement of the fish—his rise at any passing natural, and the turn and rise at the artificial—are plainly visible, is far more exciting, and requires in many respects more skill, than the *fishing of the water* as practised by the wet-fly fisherman.

CHAPTER III.

HOW TO CAST.

CASTING should be defined as placing the fly, which is at the end of the collar, in a desired spot, in a desired manner, and at a desired moment.

There are at least five distinct styles of casting, which should be understood by every dry-fly fisher. They are—firstly, the over-handed or ordinary cast; secondly, the downward cut; thirdly, the under-handed or horizontal cast; fourthly, the steeple cast; and fifthly, the dry switch.

The beginner must commence by learning the first of these, or the ordinary over-handed cast. Perhaps the easiest way for him to acquire it is to place his elbow on a gate, or even a table, so as to commence at once by using his wrist and fore-arm only. At the commencement he must content himself with only a short length of line, and it is essential that he should thoroughly master the art of casting this short length before attempting anything longer. The rod should be grasped tightly in the right hand, with the thumb, or thumb and forefinger, extended up the butt. The more usual plan is to grip the rod with

PLATE I.

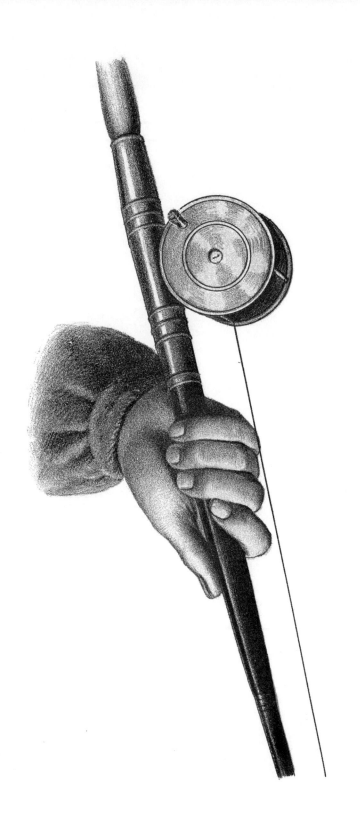

GRIP OF THE ROD.

Leighton Brothers. *Lith.*

D.Moul, del.

the thumb up the butt ; but many very experienced,
and notably one of the most accomplished dry-fly
fishermen of the present day, who uses his thumb
and forefinger for this purpose, claim some advantage
for this grip, as enabling them to direct the fly with
greater precision than with the more usual method,
illustrated on Plate I.

Holding the fly in the left hand, with a short length
of line out, wave the rod back in a curve shaped somewhat like a horse-shoe, at the same time feeling the
weight of the line with the tip of the rod, and letting
go the fly. Wait until the weight of the short line
—say five yards—just commences to bend the top
of the rod backwards before making the forward cast,
noting, however, not to carry the hand much farther
back than the perpendicular. In fact, this may be
taken as a golden rule in all styles of casting.
When the weight of the line behind is only just sufficient to bend the rod-top backwards, or, in other
words, when the line is just felt behind, return
it forwards with a slightly increased velocity of
swing. Lower the point of the rod as the line
comes forward, and see that it is extended at the
level of about one yard over the water, and then
check the forward motion. Carefully note the time of
casting, like music, counting 1, 2, back—3 forward.
It will be found that the time will vary but little
for short or long casts ; but the longer the cast, the
farther the line will extend backwards, and the
loop turning over it forwards will also be longer.

Plate II. shows the position and shape of the line when the hand has been carried back, and just before casting; Plate III. illustrates the appearance of the line when the hand has been brought part of the way forwards in the act of casting; and Plate IV. the form of the line and position of the hand when the forward motion has been completed. To these plates of casting I would invite the careful attention of my readers, because they are not in any way fancied or fanciful illustrations of what any one wishing to prove his own particular theory may think he has seen, but are actual reproductions of instantaneous photographs taken for the purpose of illustrating this work; and to the photographers, Messrs. Elliott & Fry, I must tender my hearty congratulations at the success of their work in this direction.

I would also particularly call the reader's attention to the fact that these photographs, one and all, go to destroy the theories which have been written from time immemorial in all books on fly-fishing as to the form taken by the line behind the fisherman. Over and over again it has been written, *You must wait until the line is extended in a straight line behind you before attempting to return.* This position cannot in any style of casting with a line of any appreciable length occur, and it is only because in those early days there were no scientific means of reproducing an accurate view that this theory was started. Its continuation is due to the fact that, unfortunately, by far the majo-

PLATE II.

D.Moul, del.

OVERHANDED CAST—*Backward Position.*

Leighton Brothers, *Lith.*

rity of authors simply copy, from what they deem
to be good authorities, theories which have been
before enunciated, and give them a further stamp
of veracity without taking the trouble to ascertain
for themselves that they are anything but fiction.

In the *dry switch* the length of line from the
reel to the fly was about 10 yards. In all the
other casts about 12 to 15 yards were used, and in
connection with these it should be noted that from
the transparent nature of the gut and the increased
velocity of the end of the line, an exposure of even
the 150th part of a second failed to leave a definite
trace of the three yards of gut collar on the negatives.
From a desire for extreme accuracy I have forborne
to supply this deficiency. It must also be remembered
that the foreshortening of the curves conveys an impression of a shorter line than is actually being used.

With the ordinary over-handed cast, in throwing
a long line the upper arm will come into use in
addition to the wrist and fore-arm, as the angler will
have to feel the line of the backward cast through
the arc of a larger circle. The force required to
propel various lengths of line without over-casting
or under-casting, and only just extending the line,
varies directly with every yard of line used (the
first of these terms meaning the use of too much,
and the other too little, power to extend). This in-
structive adaptation of the power to cast, of cause to
effect, constitutes the whole secret of how to cast well.

These fundamental rules apply with equal force

D

not only to dry-fly fishing and to wet-fly fishing, but
to all the various methods of casting enumerated
in the foregoing pages. The two essential points to
be attended to are, in fact, an exact appreciation of
the force to be used, and correct timing, and these are
the secrets of effective and elegant casting. It must
always be remembered that hearing much sound proceed from a rod making a cast is an indication of
unnecessary force being used; and it may be laid
down as an axiom that nine anglers out of ten use
far more force than is required for the throw, and that
excess of force only does harm. In all over-handed
casting, note particularly that the hand should never
be carried backwards far beyond the perpendicular.
As a general rule, the great fault in casting made by
beginners is in not giving sufficient time behind.

Many men who can cast a great distance and
throw a *pretty fly*, do it in so awkward a manner as
to detract very much from the pleasure experienced
in seeing their performance, and it is as easy to
cultivate a good style from the commencement as it
is difficult to cure an ugly style by any amount of
lessons after having once acquired it. A tyro can
do no better than get a friend, who can cast, to start
him in the right road, which he can do at first by
standing close behind the pupil; and, grasping the
hand holding the rod, with his fore-arm lying close
over his pupil's, guide the cast, counting at the same
time " one, two, three," until his pupil appears to
have acquired a good idea of the timing and motions.

PLATE III.

OVERHANDED CAST—*Coming Forward.*

Leighton Brothers, *Lith.*

D.Moul. del.

He should then stand clear of him on the left-hand side, criticising each cast, carefully impressing upon him the necessity of giving plenty of time between the casts, and explaining to him what fault in the motion of the rod caused the corresponding defect in the fall of the line.

After a few days of this practice, which should, if possible, be made over water, or, if water is not available, over a lawn, the tyro can be left to his own devices for a few days, when he can practise until his wrist is tired, at which time, however, he should be cautioned always to stop and rest. After a few weeks' interval, the teacher may look at him, praise and encourage where possible, point out any faults, whether of style or execution, and nip them in the bud. At the end of a fortnight an apt pupil should be sufficiently efficient to try his hand at an easy stream, where, if he has got it in him, the killing of a fish or two will make him a life votary of the charming pursuit.

Drying the fly is merely a repetition of the cast made in the afore-stated method, only that the fly, instead of being allowed to touch the water, is re-covered in the air, and the action is repeated five or six times. Note, too, that the longer the line, the farther the fly has to travel, and hence the more rapidly it is dried. Another point to remark is, that, when thoroughly dry, the fly will not soak up water nearly so fast as a half-dried one; and the fly, there-fore, should not be allowed to get water-logged, as it takes a very long time and very considerable exertion under these circumstances to dry it perfectly, thirty or forty false casts with a very long line being insufficient to make it float three or four yards, especially on fast water. The over-handed cast, it may be noted, is chiefly useful for light or up-stream winds.

The next two methods of casting, the downward cut and the under-handed cast, are specially useful for casting into or against the wind, and except in a gale, any fisherman who cares to take the trouble of mastering these two methods of casting can, after a little perseverance and careful attention to detail, render himself practically independent of the direction of the wind. If he finds himself unable to get the line out in either of these ways when casting against the wind, he must try less force and give more time behind. If still unsuccessful, he must shorten his gut collar by removing from it some few strands of the coarse end, and if the weather should be very rough, and he is still unable to force his fly into the wind, he must still further shorten the gut at the fine end; and in very rough weather it is well to note that a slight set back of the line on the water is not so very important, so long as it does not curl over on itself.

In the downward cut the fly is returned by the ordinary over-handed motion, and in the act of throwing, when the arm attains the angle of 45 degrees with the level of the water, it should be extended to full - length forwards, the knuckles

PLATE IV.

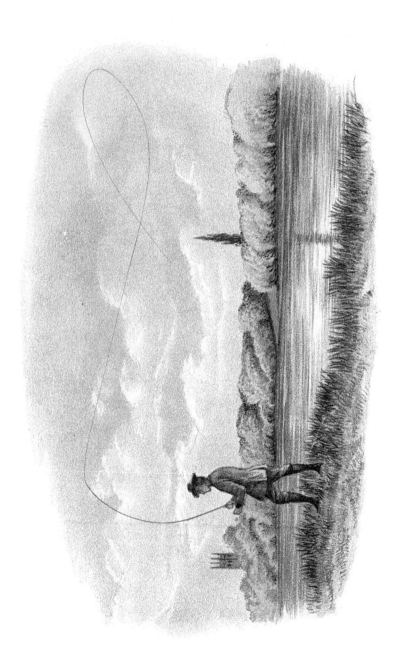

OVERHANDED CAST—*Forward Position.*

Leighton Brothers, *Lith.*

D. Moul, del.

turned downwards, and a drawing circular cut in towards the body must be made as the line is delivered, the elbow being slightly raised at the same moment, and the point of the rod brought down to the level of the water. This position is illustrated on Plate V. If this downward cut is made too soon, the whole of the line will be blown back in coils. If too late, a heavy splash on the water will be the result. If time and force are quite right—and again remember no great force is required—the line will extend itself in the teeth of the wind, the fly going out nearly straight, and the back motion of the cut pulling the slack line back, and the result of the backward motion will not really be more than the check used in the ordinary cast. The downward cut is a difficult cast to describe, and a difficult cast to attain, but it is an invaluable one when throwing against a strong wind, especially when the grass is high behind the angler, under which conditions it is at times quite impossible to use the next method, which I will now describe.

The under-handed cast, as the second method of throwing against the wind is called, is only acquired after considerable practice and perseverance, but is, as a general rule, to be preferred to the over-handed cast, and hence should be used wherever practicable. Although at the first glance in the case of one accustomed to the ordinary over-handed cast it may appear difficult to accomplish the action of returning and

throwing under-handed, yet, when once acquired, no
other method of casting into the wind is to be compared to it, especially as the motion of the rod is
far less visible to the fish.   The whole secret consists
in keeping the rod in a nearly horizontal position,
and moving it, whether returning or throwing, in a
line parallel to the surface of the water.   If, while
drying the fly, the hand holding the rod is raised
when returning, the action of the wind is very apt
to force the line back too quickly, and the fly may
be cracked off.   If sufficient time is not given behind, or, in other words, if the cast is made too soon,
in this, as in every other style of casting, the fly is
also cracked off.   If in the act of casting the hand
is raised, the force of the adverse wind on the line
prevents the fly from going out in the desired direction, and it is curled back on the reel-line, in which
position no highly-educated fish is likely to look at
the fly.   If in the act of casting the hand is unduly
lowered, the effect is a decided splash on the water.
If in returning the hand is lowered—an almost impossible action—the fly is generally securely hooked
to a blade of grass on the bank.   Hence, to make
this cast, the horizontal position of the rod moving
parallel to the water is absolutely necessary.

I have illustrated in Plate VI. the position of the
line at the moment that the rod-point is carried
to the farthest point back; in Plate VII. the
moment when the rod-point has travelled half-
way through the arc; and in Plate VIII. the forward

PLATE V.

DOWNWARD CUT—*Forward Position.*

position or finish of the cast. Continual practice, and the presence of a friend to correct faults which are frequently invisible to the fisherman himself are the best, nay, the only means of learning the action. At every opportunity, and in every possible place, this cast should be patiently persevered in.

Although naturally preferable, yet the river is not an absolute necessity, as the cast can be practised in a field or on a lawn. It must be borne in mind that the primary difficulty consists in overcoming the natural tendency to raise the hand holding the rod; and the next point is to get over the severe cramp in the hand, wrist, and fore-arm, which is caused either by bringing a new set of muscles into play, or by straining in a different direction to the accustomed one those muscles which have been hitherto used in the ordinary mode of casting. This method is especially useful when casting across wind to a fish feeding under the opposite bank, or under overhanging boughs, if they are not too low. It may also be advantageously employed in fishing a place where the trees are growing on the angler's own bank; and in this case it is necessary to remember that the rod-point should be as far as possible kept over the water while drying the fly, and that the line should be returned under and delivered over the rod-point. Above all, note where the bushes or trees are situated, and avoid them. A step to one side or the other will, as a rule, save the fly from touching them; so, look back at the

line when drying the fly, and see where it touches
in the first false cast or two, and correct before
absolutely putting the fly on the water; and even
if it should be caught behind, it will invariably be
low down within your reach, so that you can recover
the fly and save a smash.

Accuracy of direction is, however, far more difficult to attain in the under-handed cast than in any
other style of throwing; and this is due to the fact
that the rod-point, and consequently the fly, travels
in the arc of a circle or ellipse across the point to
which the fly is directed, and not in a straight line
down on it, as in the case of the over-handed
cast. Having once fairly mastered these difficulties,
the angler will find that he has not only acquired
the art of throwing a fairly long line in a manner
which makes it unlikely for the waving of the rod to
be visible to the fish, that he has not only at the same
time practically rendered himself independent of the
direction and of the force of the wind, so long as it
is short of a gale, but, strange to relate, too, his fly
will in the majority of instances land on the water
cocked or floating with its wings up in their natural
position—a most important point when dealing with
very shy fish in very clear streams.

The majority of angling books impress on the fly-
fisher the desirability of following Cotton's old
maxim to fish "fine and far off." As to the first
part there can be no doubt. To achieve success in
the present day the lower end of the gut collar, for

PLATE VI.

Leighton Brothers. *Lith.*

UNDERHANDED CAST—*Backward Position.*

D.Moul. del.

at least a yard from the fly, must be sufficiently fine. The thinnest of drawn gut in the longest lengths compatible with the strength required to handle the fish when hooked is an appreciable advantage in every stream, and an absolute necessity on those which are heavily fished. The finer the gut the greater, and the coarser the gut the smaller, the number of fish risen and hooked. On the other hand, the coarser the gut the greater, and the finer the gut the smaller, the relative proportion of fish killed when once hooked. In point of fact, the problem is to arrive at a thickness of gut which is sufficiently invisible to rise, and consequently hook, a fair proportion of feeding fish, and which, at the same time, is not so thin as to make it almost a certainty that too large a proportion of the hooked fish break the tackle either at the moment of striking, or when sufficient strain is put on to prevent their plunging headlong into the nearest bed of weeds.

As originally intended, no better advice could be given than the latter part of Cotton's adage, viz., to fish " far off; " but the tendency of the present age is to give a far wider signification to these words than their experienced author ever meant them to convey. To fish " far off " in the sense that you should, under all circumstances, keep yourself as much as possible out of the range of vision of a rising trout, by crouching, kneeling, or even lying down, is an axiom for the dry-fly fisher; but to fish " far off " in the sense that you should, for prefer-

ence, fix yourself in a position where you have to
keep on throwing an unnecessarily long line is
an absurdity. The shorter the cast in reason, the
greater is the probability of hooking the fish. The
action of the strike is delayed by the action of the
water on a long line. Get as well within your
distance of the fish as possible. By this is meant
that particular length of line which the angler finds
by experience he can manage to the greatest advantage, *i.e.*, not too long to cast with comfort, and
not so short that drying the fly becomes a heavy
toil; and this medium distance is *the* length of cast
to select wherever practicable. To most people it
is about ten to fifteen yards, and very frequently one
can locate oneself at this distance from the fish.

Instead of placing yourself at what you consider
the most favourable point for casting, and then
regulating your length of line to reach a fish rising
under your own bank, it is a good plan to keep
some thirty yards below, to let out the above length
of line, and dry the fly thoroughly in the air. Keeping your fly working backwards and forwards in the
air with the under-handed cast, so as not to scare
your fish by showing him the reflection of the rod
waving to and fro, work yourself in a crouching
attitude gradually into such a position that your
length of cast will cover the rise, and, above all,
bear in mind the importance of the first throw being
delicately and accurately made.

Occasionally the position of a tree, bush, or other

PLATE VII.

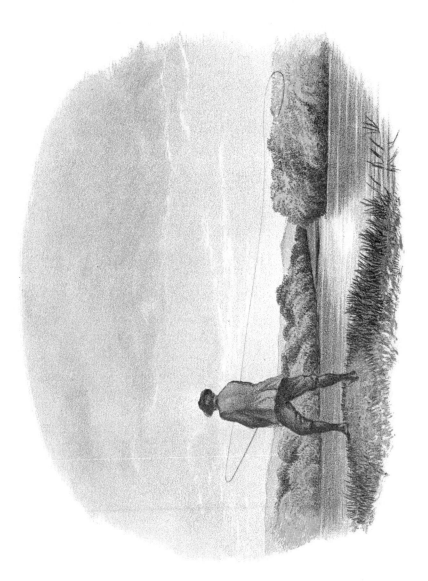

UNDERHANDED CAST—*Coming Forward.*

natural obstruction, or the shape of the river-bank, will necessitate your being much closer to your fish than you would desire, and make the cast a very short one, possibly only just the length of the gut. In such a position the dry-fly fisherman is placed at some disadvantage—first, because it is very difficult to make a clean short throw, owing to the invariable fault one makes of using far too much power. To correct this excess of force, it is a very good plan to put the left hand as well as the right to the rod (I am supposing the angler to be fishing single-handed), grasping the rod tightly in the right hand, and, just holding the spear between the left thumb and forefinger, to make the cast with both hands in this position. The effect of the left hand is merely to check the forward action, and thus prevent the exertion of undue force in the act of throwing.

A second difficulty with the very short throw is to direct the fly accurately, especially when casting against the wind, and using the taper form of line recommended in a previous chapter. Even with a short length of gut, the absence of weight in the fine end of the line increases this difficulty, and nothing but continual practice will enable the tyro to overcome this. Another practical inconvenience under such circumstances is the great exertion required to dry the fly, as many as twenty or even thirty false casts in the air being found requisite to free it thoroughly from moisture. Here again the use of both hands does, to a certain extent, distribute the strain, and will be found of considerable advantage.

There are, however, places in which one must either cast a very long line or abandon one's chance of getting fish—places in which the river is perhaps twenty-four to twenty-six yards wide, the water deep and comparatively still under your own bank, and a strong stream under the opposite one. Of course, in such a place the greater run of water, and, consequently, the greater proportion of natural flies, will float down near the farther bank, and, with the wind across or nearly across from behind the angler, every rising fish will be found there. The artificial fly, too, in such a position will fish well, and without drag. The knack of making these extra long casts is one which can be acquired without any great difficulty, and is simply invaluable to those fishing on club or subscription waters, as enabling them to give a fly to rising fish which are passed by as impossible by the majority of their brother members.

This throw, which is called the " steeple-cast," has been frequently referred to ; but many writers on the subject have, I venture to submit, failed to convey accurately the principle of it. Commencing with quite a short line, the right hand holding the rod is extended nearly straight from the shoulder, and carried up almost perpendicularly so as to lift the fly well up into the air, as if trying to clear some high obstacle immediately behind the angler, and hence the name of the " steeple-cast." While drying

PLATE VIII.

UNDERHANDED CAST—*Forward Position.*

D.Moul, del.

Leighton Brothers. *Lith.*

the fly backwards and forwards, the length of line required is gradually drawn off the reel with the left hand, and allowed to pass through the rings. Plenty of time must be given behind—in fact, it is barely possible to give too much ; and the action of throwing should be a steady swing without the slightest jerk, and very little force should be exerted in making the cast so as to allow the rod and weight of line to do the work. After the first cast has been made, the line is gathered in with the left hand in loose coils, until short enough to return with ease ; and while drying, the line is gradually liberated, a coil at each forward motion of the rod, and paid out from the left hand, the action in front being so timed as to let go a coil as the rod is in the position where the cast would have been made, and thus allow the fly to travel out in the air to the full extent of the line, but not sufficiently to let it touch the surface of the water. By the time all the coils are out the fly is thoroughly dried. If it is a very long cast, keep two or three coils in hand, and let them go when casting.

Plate IX. illustrates the position when recovering the line, Plate X. shows the form of the line when the hand is at the maximum height, and Plate XI. as it is brought down and forwards. When throwing down-wind keep the point of the rod well up in the air ; but when the direction of the wind is adverse, bring the rod-point, when making the cast, quite close to the water with a sort of modified *downward cut*. It is astonishing, again, how very little force is required to throw into wind with the *steeple-cast*. The distance to be accomplished after a little practice, by means of this style of throwing, is quite astonishing to the fisherman himself, and my friend Marryat, who is *facile princeps* in long single-handed casts, has on a calm day achieved the extraordinary feat of casting over thirty yards with an eleven-feet rod.

The switch-cast is often used amongst salmon and trout fishermen for wet-fly fishing, but there are cases in which it may be of very great service to the dry-fly fisherman. Say, for example, that there is a wall or a closely grown hedge, extending to a considerable height, a few yards behind the bank on which he is standing. On the opposite side of the river, fifteen yards off, or possibly in the middle of it, a fish is rising; and it may be most advantageous to give such a fish a well-dried fly, because he seldom sees such a thing as an artificial presented to him properly, and is consequently likely to be deluded by it. The ordinary switch, as used by the wet-fly fisher, is accomplished by drawing the line towards you on the water, and throwing the fly with a kind of roll outwards off the water—in fact, a sort of downward cut—the possibility of making the cast depending upon the fly being in the water at the moment that the rod-point is brought down; hence it is evident that the ordinary switch-cast must be made with the fly wet. The dry-fly fisherman can make a cast something like this, if there is room up and down the stream, by turning his face in that direction

PLATE IX.

D.Moul, del.

STEEPLE CAST—*Recovering the Line.*

Leighton Brothers. *Lith.*

and drying the fly in the air parallel to the course
of the river. If it is impossible to dry the fly in a
direction parallel to the course of the river, this may
be accomplished, especially when standing on a high
bank, by shortening the line considerably and drying
in a vertical direction, keeping it in front of the rod-
point. The angler then takes the dry fly between the
finger and thumb, and turning his face towards the
stream makes a false cast or two with the point of
the rod, describing a figure of 8, but still retaining
the fly between the thumb and finger. At the forward position of the rod, when the cast would in the
ordinary course of events have been made, the hold
of the fly is let go, and the line travels out to the
desired point. Care must be taken not to strike the
obstacle behind with the point of the rod, or to
entangle the line with it; and for this purpose the
action of the rod should be somewhat steepled.

This cast is certainly a very difficult one, and
whether you can accomplish it or not depends much
on the nature and distance of the obstacle behind.
The position of the hand and line at the commencement of the switch is illustrated on Plate XII.,
and the position of rod and line, just after letting
go the fly, on Plate XIII. A slight wind behind, as
in the ordinary switch, materially assists the angler,
and it is impossible to switch a dry-fly in the teeth
of a strong adverse wind.

Wherever possible the dry-fly fisherman should
cast up-stream. This may be taken as the first

fundamental principle, and often applies with equal
force to the sunk as to the floating fly.   The reasons
are so many and so obvious, that it is only necessary
to refer briefly to a few of them.

When throwing up-stream the angler is below his
fish, and the invariable position of the fish being with
head up-stream, not only for the purpose of feeding,
but for the mere mechanical process of breathing, as
carried out by the action of the gills, the angler is
in the most favourable position to keep himself
out of sight, or what an old keeper I once knew
used to call "very private." Where the stream flows
evenly, the artificial fly, when fished from below,
sails down in its natural position without drag,
following the exact direction of the current, and
presents itself to the view of the trout or grayling in
much the same way as the natural insect.   When
the fish has risen and taken the fly into his mouth,
the slightest raising of the hand, or better still the
fore-arm, drives the barb of the hook firmly home in
his jaw, or, to be precise, in my experience more
frequently into the side of his lower jaw, which is
what I should expect from the position of the hook
in a floating fly when cocked. When a large fish is
hooked it is a great advantage to the angler to be
below him, and to be able at once to commence
working him down-stream, which is at one and the
same time the best and most expeditious way to tire
him, and serves to take him farther and farther from
his home, a place where he has many more chances in

PLATE X.

STEEPLE CAST—*Backward Position.*

D. Moul, del.

Leighton Brothers, *Lith.*

his favour from his intimate daily knowledge of every weed, stone, post, or other impediment likely to assist him in cutting the connection. Where it is impossible to fish up-stream, the best direction to select is partly up and partly across. If this be impossible the cast must be made at right angles to the direction of the stream, and again, if this be impracticable, across and slightly down. When throwing across the stream attention must be paid to counteracting the tendency to drag in the manner pointed out in a subsequent chapter. Casting across and partially down is called the half-drift, and here again attention is requisite to prevent dragging by throwing a slack line, lowering the hand, or even walking along the bank as the fly floats down on the surface.

Sometimes an extra strong down-stream wind will be blowing with almost hurricane force, rendering it well-nigh impossible, or at best very difficult, to cast up against the wind, even with the under-handed cast or downward cut. Occasionally, too, there are places where, owing to natural obstructions such as trees, bushes, or a jutting promontory just in the range of the line behind the angler, there is no alternative but to drift or throw directly down-stream to a fish rising under the fisherman's own bank, or to pass him by altogether. Under such conditions, and such conditions only, is it advisable to drift to a feeding trout or grayling, although in gin-clear water such as the Hampshire chalk-streams a very small modicum of success must at the best be

E

anticipated, and no dry-fly fisherman, even the most
experienced, need be astonished at finding himself
setting down fish after fish, and perhaps not even succeeding in rising a single one during the whole day.

In considering how to drift the floating fly to
the fish, it must be remembered that in this as
in any other style of casting, the dry fly should,
as nearly as possible, imitate the position and
motion of the natural insect carried down by the
action of the current; hence the cast should be
made with the length of the line correctly judged,
and the fly accurately placed, so that it shall float
exactly over the fish's nose and travel well down
below him. In the act of casting, the hand should
be well extended, so as to be able to draw it back.
Just as the line is fully extended over the water
and at a level of quite two yards above it, the
hand holding the rod must be carried some distance
back so as to check the cast and place the artificial
—of course quite dry, cocked, and floating—well
in front of the fish, with sufficient slack line on the
water, so that by gradually lowering the hand and
point of the rod the fly will float down until well
past the fish, without the slightest stoppage or drag.
It is well to remember, too, that a fish will at times
back and take the fly as much as two yards below
where he rose. This is specially the case with
the May-fly.

Having made the cast, and the fly having drifted
down below the fish without rising him, it is evi-

PLATE XI.

STEEPLE CAST—*Coming Forward.*

D.Moul, del.

Leighton Brothers, *Lith.*

dently necessary to return the line, and the difficulty of accomplishing this in such a way as not to scare him is at best very great. In some places the whole length of line can be lifted sideways clean over the bank, quite out of his range of vision. But where this is not possible, the line must be gathered in very slowly with the left hand (supposing the rod to be held with the right), until the fly is well above the fish, when it can be slowly taken off the water, keeping the rod-point well down so that the angle of contact of the line with the water will be very obtuse and not scare the fish. With the utmost caution, however, it is very difficult to accomplish the return without rousing the suspicions of your wary quarry, and hence in this style of casting, even more than in any other, the greatest precision and delicacy are necessary in the first throw.

In club waters, which are so generally over-fished, it is not as a rule worth while to make a second drift over a trout until he has risen again. If not taken at the first attempt, and provided he does not rise again within say five minutes, it is generally as well to leave the fish and pass on to another, keeping wide of him, carefully *spotting* his position, and possibly returning to give him a further trial later in the day. A grayling, however, will frequently allow a careful and light fisherman, using the very finest of tackle, to make a second or even third cast over him, and then perhaps rise falsely, when, after a rest of a few minutes—especially if in the meantime he

has taken a natural fly or two—another cast may be
successful in securing him. The half-drift, partly
across and partly down stream, if the fly is well
checked as it is descending, and when on the water
allowed to float down without drag, is, however, frequently efficacious, especially in rough windy weather,
the angler above the fish being, of course, less
visible under such conditions. Both trout and grayling will, in such a case, often rise at and fasten to
a somewhat large fly if quite dry and cocked. I do
not think a particular pattern is of very great importance ; but for what it is worth, my own experience
gives the preference in such a case to the Wickham,
or better still, the landrail winged variety of it,
on a No. 1 or No. 2 hook. The half-drift is an
especially successful cast for grayling ; in fact,
many experienced fishermen prefer it to any other
cast for them.

One of the reasons why drifting is not generally
successful is, that the horizontal cast is often impossible, as when throwing in this way it is necessary
to cast directly down the line of the current, and as
the fly descends, to check the cast in the same direction. But with the under-handed or horizontal cast
it is manifestly impossible to effect this, as the fly
must of necessity travel round a curve something in
the shape of a semicircle or semi-ellipse. The ordinary over-handed cast then becomes almost the only
practicable one ; and in addition to the very grave
defect in this style of cast that the shadow of the

PLATE XII.

DRY SWITCH—*Commencement.*

Moul, del.

Leighton Brothers, *Lith*.

upright rod and of the line are ever moving backwards and forwards immediately over the fish and in his direct line of vision, whilst the angler is above him and also well within his sight, another and perhaps even more serious disadvantage is present, namely, that although a cocked fly is almost indispensable, it is, as shown before, only in a minority of cases possible to effect this when throwing over-hand. To sum up the position, it amounts to this : one throw, and one throw only, must be made ; and although it may happen that the several remote contingencies of placing the fly accurately and lightly on the water, of letting it drift down over the fish without drag, and floating in the vertical position or cocked, and at the same time succeeding in making the fish rise, may come off, yet in sporting parlance it is any odds against landing the treble, or rather quadruple event.

Even if all the above difficulties have been happily accomplished at the first attempt, and the fish rises and takes the fly as it reaches his nose, another serious difficulty occurs. The fish has just come open-mouthed at the fly ; it is between his capacious jaws ; to force the barb of the hook home it is necessary to strike promptly, and as the direction of the strike is coincident with the line of aperture of the fish's mouth, it must be achieved at the very moment that his lips are closed on the fly ; or, discovering the fraud practised on him, he will to a certainty open his mouth and eject the very best and most natural imitation. Even if the angler does succeed in striking at the right moment, it is not easy to do so with just sufficient force and no more. Too little force and the fish is scratched. The least trifle too much leaves the fly in his mouth, and with the line extended straight down-stream and the weight of the current on it, it is surprising how little apparent force, with the assistance of the leverage of the rod, is necessary to make a smash of the gossamer gut. Altogether, as before said, this is the most difficult and disappointing cast of any, and should never be adopted, except as a last resource where all others have been tried, and tried in vain.

PLATE XIII.

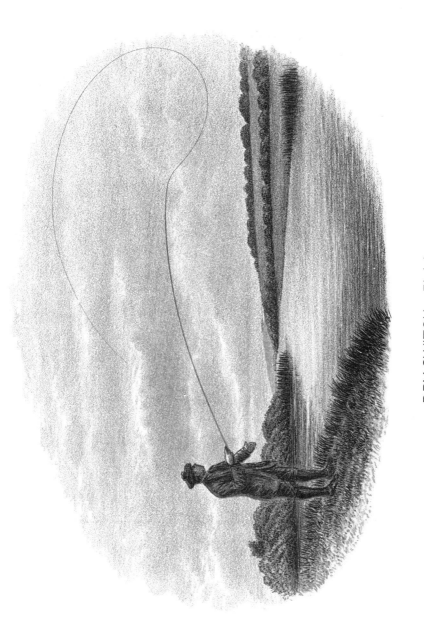

DRY SWITCH—*Finish*.

Leighton Brothers, *Lith*.

D.Moul. del.

CHAPTER IV.

WHERE TO CAST.

WITH the modern angler it may be taken as an axiom that his sport is not what is popularly called *luck*, but varies directly as his judgment; and as a corollary, it may be added that, provided he is a keen and accurate observer, his judgment will vary directly as his experience, tempered by his capacity of execution. The object of this chapter is to try and give, as far as possible, the experience of others to improve the judgment of the beginner, and to convey, where possible, hints to men of experience.

No point can possibly be of more importance than a well-grounded knowledge of *where to cast;* and it must be borne in mind that this knowledge is not intuitive, but must be acquired by marking, learning, and continuously studying the relation of the fish and his food, and striving as far as is practicable to take advantage of it. The modern school are far too much addicted to continual change of fly, often changing merely for the sake of changing, and trying imitations of the same insect, only differing slightly in size, or in the shade of the body, wings, or legs; forgetting that the fault too often lies in

their own lack of discrimination, which causes them
to select fish in unlikely or impossible places, or
offer surface food to a fish feeding on larvæ or other
forms of insect life in the middle depths or on the
bottom of the river. At the same time, it must be
admitted that colour, form, and size, or, in other
words, a fairly accurate imitation of the natural fly
on the water, is always and in every way more
likely to tempt a trout feeding on duns than some
monstrosity like nothing in nature, styled a fancy
pattern, which can only appeal to his curiosity.

Places which should be selected by the dry-fly
fisherman may be divided into three classes—firstly,
those which are affected by fish feeding freely, owing
to a large proportion of the natural insects being
carried to or past them by the action of the stream
or wind; secondly, those where, owing to difficulties
inherent to the situation, the artificial fly is seldom
presented to the rising fish in the same position and
following the same rate and direction of progress as
the living fly; thirdly, places where the inherent
shyness of the fish is decreased by frequent sight of
human beings, or by some other abnormal cause.

Of the first of these three classes a trout rising
close to a bank (and here perhaps it is as well to
note that grayling, as a rule, are not found rising in
such a position) is generally a large one, who chooses
for his feeding-ground a spot where almost off the
sedges themselves, from under a hollow bank, or
from the boards of camp-shutting, he can pick up

a good meal with a minimum of effort or exertion. A typical fish to cast for is a trout feeding under the left-hand bank of the river (looking up-stream), thus giving the angler a right-handed throw, with the rod over the water. The stream should be slow and steady, the wind blowing very slightly; in fact, only sufficient to make a slight ripple on the surface, and in direction towards that bank. There should be a fair amount of fly hatching, but not too much. The fish should be lying near the top of the water taking every natural fly coming over him. The sun should be in the fisherman's face, and not too bright. The fisherman should, of course, be on the same bank as the fish, and should be able to get within a reasonable distance, so as to cast for him with a comparatively short line, say from ten to fifteen yards. On the plan appended to this chapter (Plate XIV.) such places are indicated by the letters *a*, *a*, *a*.

One feeding under the opposite bank is usually able to see you before you are at an angle of 45° with him, or fairly within casting distance. In a wide stream, where the current is slow and moderately even, but the strongest part of it runs close to the opposite bank (Plate XIV. *b*), this may be considered a favourable spot if the angler will keep low and fish the underhanded cast, as the natural fly drifts there, and the artificial fishes well and without drag. Even if the wind is dead down-stream, so long as it is very light, such a place is not to be despised when found. Unfortunately, however, it is not often found in practice.

At every turn of the river there is generally a succession of points, close to the bank, to which every floating object, animate or inanimate, is carried by the set of the current and wind, and the heaviest and easiest fish, as a rule, take up these enviable positions (Plate XIV. c). Subject to exception, to be hereafter treated of, these are, as a rule, places where one should cast. It must always be remembered that when feeding close to the bank a trout is generally less liable to be scared by a small mistake, and even less liable to notice it, as the eye nearest to the bank is invariably in deep shade, and probably at the same time is ever intent on watching for edible morsels passing between it and the margin of the stream. It is sometimes a very deadly plan to place the fly on the bank, and with a slight movement persuade it to drop on the water. This comes off best on short grass, as the fly does not usually get hung up in it. Sedges, however, are dangerous. If the hook should get caught up, take the line in your hand and draw gently, but do not on any account try to extricate it by striking or jerking with the rod-point. Every angler of experience has occasionally killed a trout blind of one eye rising close under the bank, and in such a case it may safely be predicted that the fish is rising with the blind eye towards the middle of the stream and the perfect one against the bank.

On a well-kept shallow—that is, one on which a fair proportion of the weed is left uncut in bars, and

in which bright patches of clean gravel alternate
with banks of weeds—every fish feeding on fly will
take up his station over these gravel patches (*see*
Plate XIV. *d*), and some of the cleverest fishermen occasionally float a dry fly *on spec* over the best-
looking of such places if even they fail to see a sign
of a rise, knowing that if a fish is there he must be in
position, and ready and likely to take advantage of
any unexpected treat provided for him.   In all water,
whether deep or shallow, with plenty of weeds scientifically cut so as to leave clear runs between them,
the feeding fish lie mostly on the tails of the weed-
patches, where the water commences to slacken, and
are partly covered by the weeds or bank-edge, and
in such a position rise with confidence to every passing insect; and when disturbed by an imprudent
passer-by, or even pricked, merely glide into the
depths of the weeds close to them, and soon come
on the feed again (such places are shown on Plate
XIV. *e, e*); while, on the other hand, in an open
bare piece of water utterly denuded of shelter, when
alarmed they bolt off for twenty or thirty yards,
starting in their headlong rush any other fish in
the vicinity.

At the tail of a rough run, where the water
commences to deepen and become smooth (Plate
XIV. *f*), where the fly, after being whirled over
and over and swept down at a great pace, recovers
its equilibrium and sails calmly and slowly down
on the deep glide, there is often a specially good fish

waiting to be tempted if the first cast is delicately made and the artificial fly floats down cocked.

In very hot weather the hatch of fly in the middle of the day is as a rule sparse, but if at such a time an occasional quiet ring or a mere bubble is espied in a shady nook or under an overhanging bank, a fish there should be selected in preference to any feeding in the full glare of the midday sun as likely to be large as well as sometimes unsuspecting.

In large deep eddies the best fish often rise very quietly in curious positions, generally with their heads directed apparently down-stream, although this is, of course, only apparent, as in this case the flies are carried round the back-eddy in the opposite direction to the general run of the river. If the eddy be large enough and the position of the rise such as to enable the angler to make a wide circuit *up-stream* in order to get *below* the fish, and, throwing up the eddy, place his fly so that it drifts accurately over the fish, while the reel-line remains in the back-eddy so as not to produce any drag, the spot is a favourable one to try. (Such places are shown on Plate XIV. *g.*) The foregoing are all positions to be selected as those in which fish are naturally prone to feed.

With respect to the second category, or spots where it is difficult to place a fly, such as under the boughs of trees hanging close down to the water, or where it is only possible to fish with an under-handed cast, or even with a left-handed under-handed cast, or close to the knotted roots of trees or willows, a feeding fish should never be entirely passed over. In such a position he does not see an artificial fly floating over him cocked, without drag, and delivered without splash half a dozen times in a season, and when he does the result is a rise, if not a kill.

Dry your fly up and down the stream and cast across from the hand (*dry switch*) in situations where there is a high bank, or bushes behind, and the water is clear. The *under-handed cast* is also useful where there are trees behind with boughs not very low on the water. Look back when drying the fly and see that the line when returned behind you works clear of bushes or trees. If the fly should catch it is sure to be low down, where you can un-hook it by hand. Where you see a fish feeding in a difficult place under a bush you are not unlikely to catch the gleam of a portion of a gut collar hanging in the bush. Note the danger to avoid it, and col-lect the remains of some other fisherman's collar; the fly at the end of it may often give you a useful hint as to the patterns used by the local talent—a hint they are not always willing to convey by word of mouth.

Again, you are out on a boisterous day, and the first fish you see rising is in a foul corner, where the wind is in every way contrary. Nineteen out of twenty fishermen pass such a fish as impossible. But the twentieth, grateful for the chance, setting his teeth, grasping his rod, and shortening the gut by two or three links, by means of the under-handed cast, or if that be impracticable, the downward cut, gives the hungry trout a chance of which he is not slow to avail himself.

Some days, again, especially on a club or subscription water, you will notice that your brother fishermen have started early so as to be before you, and have walked up the windward bank. You reflect that all the feeding fish that they, or possibly you, can reach are most likely killed or spoiled before you can get up to them. You decide to walk up as quickly as possible to get in front of them, and then all day long you and they are engaged in a breathless sort of race, one trying to get above the other, with the result that all alike get little or no sport. This is a great mistake, and the next time it happens try exactly the opposite tactics. Give them a good start, walk leisurely up the lee bank, cast a short line, and throwing *into* the wind, try all the fish you can see rising under your own bank. Do not be afraid of the work of casting against the wind, because this, as shown in a previous chapter, is not altogether difficult when you know how it is to be done; and I venture to prophesy that very possibly at the end of the day you may find yourself with a better bag, and generally more contented than any of them.

Also note fish rising under the *lee* of the windward bank, especially if the current sets there, as the natural flies remain in this *glass edge* out of the wind. Fishermen looking across will often walk over them and set them down. They soon come on the feed again, and you can walk leisurely up this windward bank and pick up a bag behind them. There are usually two glass edges where the wind is across the stream, one under each bank; that on the windward side is the part protected from the force of the wind by the height of the bank, and that on the lee side is produced by the back-eddy of wind thrown off the lee bank counteracting the force of the breeze blowing directly towards that bank.

The third class of places to select, namely, those in which the fish are rendered less shy by some abnormal cause, are as a general rule neglected by the majority of anglers, as, for example, the extreme ends or limits of a water. If at the lower end, most fishermen are far too impatient to get on, opining that if the fish are not feeding well there, they may perchance be farther afield; and as to the upper boundary, that generally is never reached if the fishery be of any great extent. My advice is, never neglect these positions, and never leave rising fish to go in search of others in what you fancy are more likely places. As a rule, if the fish are taking well in one part of the water they are taking equally well in others, and *vice versâ*. If you are starting at the lower end do not be in a hurry; wait there until the fish begin rising, and try the fish there. On the other hand, if you are cold and want exercise to restore the circulation, walk briskly to the extreme upper end of the water, and there again wait for the rise, and fish it.

In portions of a river along which a public footpath or roadway runs trout very soon become accustomed to the sight of human beings, and are as a consequence comparatively tolerant of their intrusive curiosity. They are then not so easily scared, and if scared when rising, are not long in returning to their habitual feeding-place to resume their interrupted meal. A fish rising immediately above a bridge or a hatch is never very shy, and, besides, is very seldom fished for; the sapient angler opines that it is hopeless, as the trout will bolt down through the bridge or through the hatch the moment he is hooked. If it be a bridge, he does usually run down *under*, but not *through*, and there he remains in the shadow of the bridge until by the continued strain of the rod you have drowned him and can land him at your leisure. Even if, once in a way, he does make a clean bolt through it and smashes you, or come unhooked, even then perhaps it is better to have hooked and lost your fish than never to have hooked one all day long.

Never hold a fish very hard when bolting through an arch of a bridge. If he is eased his natural tendency is to work up after the first rush, and then perhaps you may coax him away from the dangerous locality. In the case of a hatch, if a hooked fish runs through it, the rod can often be passed through point first, and the fish killed at your leisure in the hatch-hole below. With a fish rising under a bridge or at the upper end of it, either go above and drift to him with a strong down-stream wind, or, what is far better, where possible go below and throw up with the under-handed cast.

In very rough weather in portions of the stream which are usually smooth but are then ruffled by strong gusts of wind and perhaps occasionally lighted up by warm gleams of sunshine, fish are often seen feeding among the waves or quietly sucking in the flies dancing over the rippling surface. Such fish are generally travelling; in that case throw well above the rise, taking especial care to notice in which direction they are moving. Under such circumstances they are usually silly and unsuspecting, and should never be passed by without just one polite invitation in the shape of a floating dun perfectly dry and well cocked.

Among dry-fly fishermen the remark is often heard that a particular throw is not likely to be successful, or that a fish rising in a particular place is, practically speaking, out of danger, owing to the fact that with the particular throw or in the particular place the fly is bound to *drag*. The exact meaning of this expression is, however, only clear to a small minority of modern anglers, and as the main principle of dry-fly fishing and the success and want of success of the angler is absolutely dependent on this point, it is worthy of a proper definition. When a fly is said to be dragging, the meaning is, that it is travelling down the stream in some degree differently to the natural insect. This can occur in

F

one of three different respects; firstly, by the artificial
fly travelling more rapidly than the natural; secondly,
by its travelling more slowly than the natural; and
thirdly, owing to its drifting across the run of the
stream, in each case leaving a more or less perceptible *wake*. The natural insects under normal
conditions emerge from the covering in which they
have been enveloped in the larva or nymph state,
on the surface of the stream, float down at precisely
the same pace as the current, and follow precisely
the direction of the particular run in which they
happen to be when they reach the surface; hence
in every stream the probability of a shy fish like a
trout or grayling rising at any artificial fly which takes
a course opposed to that of the natural one is remote;
while in clear water or in rivers which are heavily
fished it may be practically considered an absolute
certainty that this remote probability will not *come
off*. When the wind is blowing very strongly across
the current, it sometimes causes the natural fly to
drag and leave a wake, and when this happens the
fish seldom or ever take it. This experience is derived
entirely from streams which are heavily fished, and
it would be interesting, as tending to show whether
this shyness is inherent in fish or the outcome of a
prolonged and advanced education, to know whether
the same thing occurs on waters where the fly-fisherman is comparatively unknown.

Now to deal with the various causes of the fly
dragging, owing to its travelling more rapidly than

the stream; and in all cases, where possible, to indicate the means of modifying or counteracting this tendency. The most usual position in which the angler is troubled by this form of dragging is where he is casting across or partially across and up the stream, and where the swiftest portion of the current is between him and the point to which he is directing his fly. In such a case throwing in the ordinary way and with a moderately straight line, the strength of the current pressing against the reel-line forces it down-stream, thus causing a pull on the fly, dragging it more or less across, but at the same time making it travel at the pace of the strongest part of the stream, or at a greater pace than the natural fly under similar conditions. The most effectual means of obviating this is to make the cast in such a way that while the fly and last yard of the gut collar lie in a direct line, the remainder of the collar and a portion of the reel-line lie on the water in a curve the convex side of which tends up the stream. The strength of the current then acting on the belly of the line and pressing it down-stream does not cause the fly to drag before it has forced the convex side of the curve into a straight line, and, if the convexity of the curve has been sufficiently pronounced, until the fly is beyond the point where the fish is rising. Of course the longer the cast and the greater the disproportion between the extreme rapidity of the current and that at the feeding-place of the fish

the sharper or more convex this curve requires to
be. To deliver the line in this curved state with
the over-handed or ordinary cast the assistance of
a slight up-stream wind is necessary; but with the
under-handed cast, it is far easier to accomplish it
with a slight down-stream wind than with one
blowing directly up or across. In such a case it
is not necessary to throw absolutely against the
wind, but merely to *cheat* it slightly; and hence,
if the angler finds the direction of his first cast is
too much into the wind, he must correct the inaccuracy in the next, either by using less force, by
easing the point of his rod in the act of delivery,
or by increasing the length of the gut collar which
he is using. If the direction of the wind is up-stream
the fisherman must take up his position on the
bank a very short distance below or even level with
the rising fish; and, to allow for the action of the
wind, the cast must be made as though his object
was to place the fly slightly *below* the fish. With a
down-stream wind it will, on the other hand, be
necessary to direct the fly towards a point slightly
above the fish.

Some natural obstruction on the bank or an
extremely long throw may render the under-handed
cast difficult, or even impossible; and on rare occasions, too, the force of the down-stream wind may
be too great to be overcome. In either of these
cases the fisherman must place himself directly
opposite to or slightly above the spot where the

fish is feeding. The ordinary over-handed cast must then be made, or if necessary, owing to the distance being very great, the steeple-cast is used, and with either of them a slight downward cut is incorporated, and at the moment that the fly has travelled out to the full extent of the line the cast is perceptibly checked and the fly lands on the water with the last yard of the gut straight, and the remainder of the gut and a portion of the reel-line in curves or loosely behind it. At the moment that the fly touches the water the hand is lowered to allow it to come over the fish before the line is sufficiently taut to cause a drag, and as remarked in a previous chapter, sometimes it is necessary for the angler to walk at the same pace and in the same direction as the fly is floating down.

When throwing across a very wide stream throughout which the current is flowing evenly there will frequently be a slight drag, especially if the line sinks; and in such a case the plan described above of placing the fly with a convex side of the curve or belly of the line inclined up-stream should be adopted, or else that of throwing a slack line. The meaning to be attached to the expression *throwing a slack line* is, that the force to be used should be a trifle more than is necessary to put the line out straight, and in making this cast the hand must be checked slightly, so that, as before, the fly and last yard of the gut are extended, while the upper part of the cast and a portion of the reel-line lie in curves or loosely on the water.

Fish, more especially grayling, often rise in a smooth place immediately above a swift run, and in such a position a straight cast made up-stream from below lays the reel-line on the hardest of the run, and the fly, being on the comparatively still glide above, is dragged down by it. To avoid this drag, the place must either be fished from above with the half-drift, or from below with a good deal of slack line on the run, so that the fly is below the fish before it commences to drag.

Another very favourite position for a rising fish is a small eddy or a slow-running bay under the bank, where most of the natural fly is carried by the stream. Both trout and grayling, especially large ones, being naturally inclined to get their food with as little work as possible, show a preference for spots into which the fly is carried by the action of the stream or wind, and where it is almost stationary, or at most moves very slowly. If the eddy is so strong that the natural insects drift in the opposite direction to the general run of the stream, the fish lies with his head down-stream, or rather down what is the general run of the stream; and if this happens in a very small space it is almost impossible to fish it without drag. Where, however, instead of an eddy there is a mere slackening of the stream, the difficulty may be overcome by putting plenty of slack line so that no drag takes place until the fly is past the fish.

With a strong up-stream wind, a fish rising directly above the angler is apparently in a very favourable position ; but it must be remembered that the cast is a straight one, that is, that at the moment the fly lands on the water the line is extended to its uttermost, and hence any slight inequality of the stream causes the fly to commence dragging, and to continue dragging until it has travelled far enough to cause a slight slackness in the line. Anglers, from ignorance or want of observation, are often surprised at finding difficulty in rising fish in such a position, while the remedy is a very simple one. To obviate the drag, keep the point of the rod well in the air when casting, and immediately after the fly has fallen on the water drop the hand, and naturally with it the rod-point, so as to slacken the line and remove the strain, which would otherwise cause a drag. The foregoing are probably the only positions in which the artificial fly travels more rapidly than the natural.

An artificial fly travels more slowly than the natural when throwing across, or partially across, the stream in places where the upper portion of the gut cast or the reel-line lies on an eddy. A slack line will to a certain degree prevent this; but such a place is never easy to fish, and the angler must not have great hopes of killing in such a position except, perhaps, on a rough or rainy day, or in

water slightly coloured, or late in the evening.
With a very strong down-stream wind the natural
fly itself is occasionally forced along at a greater
speed than the normal pace of the current. In
such a case the artificial fly drifts more slowly than
the natural, but in rivers that are much fished or
where trout are fairly well educated I do not find
that they are very prone even to take the natural
when drifting faster than the stream ; and I at-
tribute this to the fact that under such conditions even the natural fly leaves a slight wake on
the water ; and hence I would venture the opinion
that this action of the artificial fly must not be
considered as dragging; in fact, it is questionable
whether under such conditions the fish will not
at times take the imitation in preference to the
living insect.

The artificial fly drifts across the natural set of
the stream under the following circumstances :—
Firstly, when throwing across, or across and partially down, as soon as the line commences to
tighten. This particular form of dragging can sometimes be delayed until the fly is past the fish by
easing the hand and dropping the rod-point towards
the water, or sometimes by walking slowly down-
stream. Secondly, in deep pools through which
a number of irregular cross currents or eddies flow.
Such places are as a rule very disappointing, especially in long casts, as the line is subject to the action
of several of these currents, and, excepting in rough

weather or late in the evening, or perhaps when
quite dark, should be avoided; if, however, fish
cannot be found rising elsewhere, some little time
may be devoted to what is far more likely to be
educating than catching them. Thirdly, where the
water at the head or any other part of a shallow
commences to widen, the stream usually divides into
a number of fan-shaped runs, and a natural fly of
course would drift down the run on which it
happened to be when emerging from the nymph
envelope. In the case of the artificial, however,
if there happen to be one or more of these runs
between the angler and the place where the fish is
rising, it is dragged across the natural flow of the
current, and hence, it may be inferred, will not be
taken. If in such a place it is practicable to wade
and stand immediately below the rising fish, on the
edge of the very fan-run in which he is feeding,
well and good; there is every chance of getting
the fish. If, again, by standing well above the
fish and half drifting to him, the fly can be got
past him without drag, there is again a fair chance
of killing him; but if it is too deep to wade, and
the distance from the bank is too great for the
second alternative above defined, the place is, to all
practical intents and purposes, an impossible one,
and the fish is safe.

In indicating places which should, as a general
rule, be avoided, it must be clearly understood that
the idea is to give a few practical hints, especially to

the younger generation of dry-fly fishermen, to assist
them in judging whether, under ordinary conditions,
a fish feeding in a particular spot is a *killable* one or
not. At the same time, in streams where fishermen
are not often seen, and where the floating fly is
almost unknown—in fact, where the education of
the fish has not been carried to a high standard—
the silly ones will occasionally take well in such
places, and upset all the preconceived scientific
theories on the subject. In the same way, in a
gale of wind, with the surface lashed into heavy
waves, or during heavy rain or hailstorms, or when
nearly dark, these unlikely places may, even in the
shyest of chalk-streams, be tried with success.

To recapitulate briefly, a fish rising in any place
where the fly is likely to drag is a difficult
one to tempt. Such places are where the strongest
of the current is between the angler and the
feeding-place of the fish (Plate XIV. *v*); where
throwing across a very wide stream, even where the
current is uniform (the use of the slack-line, the
bowed cast with belly of line up-stream, or the half-
drift will prevent or delay the drag in these positions); a small eddy or bay (Plate XIV. *w*); deep
eddying pools (with some exceptions); a smooth
glide at the head of a run (Plate XIV. *x*); or
amongst the fan-shaped runs where wading is impossible, as shown on Plate XIV. *y*.

In summer-time there are on most shallows portions covered with a very close, compact growth of

PLATE XIV.

WHERE TO CAST.

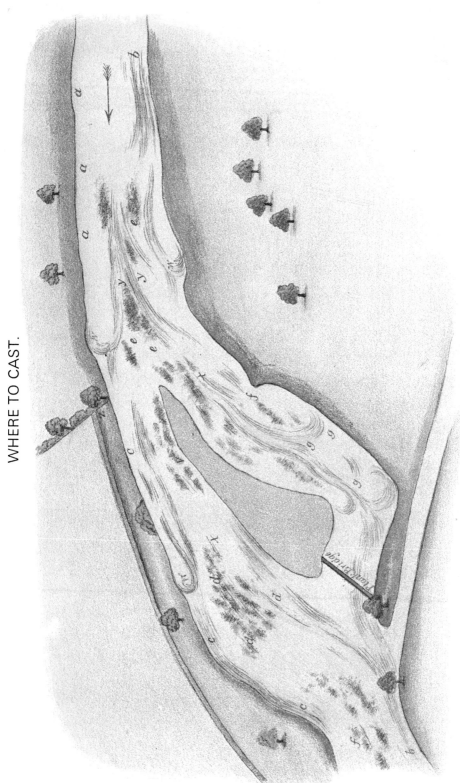

quite short, bright green weeds, and for the purpose of briefly referring to such places it may be well to borrow friend Marryat's terse cognomen for them— *celery beds.* Often and often trout are apparently rising well over these celery beds, and inexperienced anglers too often waste a considerable time in trying to tempt them. At first their inability to get even an offer induces them to try another pattern of fly, which in its turn is changed for another, and still another. At length, in despair, the fisherman makes cast after cast in rapid succession, generally not even taking the trouble to dry his fly, until, utterly worn out and with every muscle of his hand and arms aching severely, he abandons the attempt. In point of fact, fish in such a position are rarely, if ever, taking duns or winged flies of any sort, but are picking up any little larvæ, caddis, shrimps, snails, or other molluscs drifting off the weed.

This is no mere theoretical assertion, but the result of continual practical experiment, obtained by minute examination, day after day and year after year, of the contents of the stomachs of both trout and grayling taken under such conditions. Methinks the reader may with reason exclaim against the inconsistency of advising him in the first instance to avoid such places, and in the very next sentence referring to an examination of the contents of the stomachs of fish—an examination which, in the natural course of events, must have been preceded by their capture. True; but mark how this has been accomplished in nearly every case. When no rising fish could be found in a more favourable situation, the plan adopted has been to put up either a gold-ribbed hare's ear (one of the best general patterns of duns known) or an orange bumble ; in either case to fish quite dry, throwing only at long intervals, and altogether resting the fish from time to time, until at length occasionally a rise has secured the trout or grayling. What the fish mistake the hare's ear or bumble for is mere conjecture. The hare's ear, possibly, is taken for a dun just emerging from the nymph envelope, and the bumble does certainly bear some faint resemblance to one of the orange tinted fresh-water shrimps. The above remarks as to fish feeding over "celery beds" apply in a lesser degree to fish rising in any part of the water, deep or shallow, swift or still, over heavy banks of submerged weed.

The inexperienced dry-fly fisherman should generally avoid places in which the stream is very swift. Such places are difficult, for two reasons; firstly, because it is not easy to time the action of the hand so as to raise the rod just quickly enough to keep the slack line off the water without dragging the fly, (and with the slack on the water one may generally expect to miss the fish altogether, or at best only to hook it lightly); secondly, because fish in a very swift run do not as a general rule feed in the most rapid portion of it, but take up their position just above the hardest part of it, in which case the artificial fly must infallibly drag. There are nearly always fish feeding immediately below a wide plank bridge or wooden-trunk carrier, and every fisherman passing by is irresistibly impelled to study their movements. As a natural sequence he crouches down, creeps slowly below them, gets into position, dries his fly carefully, and takes a cast or two. How very seldom he is successful, and how rarely fish in such a place are easy to kill though really taking well! Is it because they are so frequently tried for? This may be, although I confess I doubt it, and am inclined to think that from some as yet unexplained effect of light and shade either the gut, the hook, or any little imperfection of shape or colour in the fly itself is in some way brought prominently to the notice of the fish, looking upwards against the dead background of the bridge or carrier.

When only rising moderately well, fish in deep black-looking pools may as a general rule be considered unpromising, although here again an exception may be made at dusk, when, if no other rising fish can be descried, a few minutes may often be profitably devoted to them. At times, in such a place, a considerable number of fish are seen rising in close proximity, and after a number of casts, or until the angler succeeds in catching one, he is in doubt as to whether they are salmonidæ or not. If he can secure one, and finds it is a dace, there is no occasion to go on, as probably they are all dace; at the same time it is frequently the habit of an angler to pronounce fish that he cannot catch in a trout stream to be dace—and they certainly are very difficult to catch, and at times it is a convenient excuse for not killing a big trout.

An example of this I can give on a club water well known on the Test. Two members starting in the morning saw two fish rising quietly under the shade of an old elm. Piscator No. 1 settled down to try them, and his companion walked on. An hour or so later Piscator No. 1 joined Piscator No. 2, and with some emphasis exclaimed at the presence of this wretched vermin in a trout stream, imagining and stating that he had wasted his valuable time in vainly trying to tempt two big dace. Piscator No. 2, a somewhat incredulous but experienced follower of the craft, made a mental note of the exact position of these two dace, and determined to devote a few minutes to them on his way home. When comparing bags, Piscator No. 1 was rather disgusted to find that two trout weighing somewhere about seven pounds were the dace which he had failed to beguile in the morning: I mention this to show how difficult it is to differentiate the rise of dace from that of trout, and how unsafe it is to be quite positive in these cases. As a general rule, a number of fish rising abreast of each other are probably dace. Trout feeding close together usually hunt one another, as also do grayling, but not so decidedly as trout. Dace generally travel in shoals and feed in shoals, while trout feeding are more often in position one behind the other.

Sometimes grayling, and large grayling too, may be seen rising in close proximity in these deep, still pools. As a rule, careful scrutiny will enable the angler to distinguish them from coarse fish, from the curious way in which when breaking the surface they show their dorsal fins, and at times, too, all doubt is removed by catching sight of the adipose fin, which latter, it must be mentioned, is an unmistakable index only existing in members of the salmon family.

A corner or bend into which the wind sets directly up-stream, and into which every fly floats, looks an inviting one, but it should be borne in mind that on a club or subscription water no passing angler can by any possibility fail to catch sight of fish feeding in such a place; and if they have been sedulously fished for only a few minutes previously, it is surprising how soon their suspicions are aroused, and how small a mistake will *set them down*. This same argument applies to any portion of a piece of water held in high repute by our brother fishermen, either as a taking place or as one containing an extraordinarily large number of fish, and my advice to the thinking angler is to pass such places by. At best he is far more likely to add to the already far advanced education of the fish than to the contents of his bag. When fishing for trout in hot calm weather, portions of the river in the full glare of the sun, especially in mid-stream, should be avoided. But, at the same time, it must be remembered that the largest and freest rising grayling are usually to be found in such places, and this, I take it, is one of the most salient points of difference between the feeding-places affected by the grayling and by the trout.

Wherever the bank is raised much above the level of the river (and such a place is shown on Plate XIV. z), the angler is more visible to the fish, and is hence placed at a great disadvantage; and if it be just as the shadows are commencing to lengthen in the evening on the western bank, it is often impossible, when standing up, to approach within twenty-five or thirty yards of the stream without scaring every fish over whom the fisherman's shadow passes. If no fish can be found rising in a more favourable place, it is sometimes possible to get into position by crawling slowly to the bank on all-fours, taking especial care that the shadow is not thrown beyond the edge of the sedges on the side of the river nearest to you.

Above all, when stalking a fish do not forget to move slowly. A quick motion is not only more visible to the fish, and hence more likely to scare him, but a quick footstep causes more motion of the bank, which communicates vibration to the water, and, with it, an intimation to the fish of the angler's presence. Having stalked into position, and, I presume, the fly being thoroughly dry, crouch down as much as possible, throw with the under-handed cast only, and be careful not to raise the point of the rod, nor to throw its shadow across the rising fish, either when throwing or subsequently when drying your fly, as neglect of this advice must invariably reveal the fisherman's presence to the well-educated fish. With these precautions, it is sometimes possible to float a fly over such a place without setting the fish down; but, at the same time, it is astonishing how small a movement will scare him, a fact which will usually be brought home to the fisherman by the heavy furrow caused by the headlong flight of the frightened trout to the innermost recesses of the nearest bed of weeds.

G

CHAPTER V.

WHEN TO CAST.

IF the first throw over a rising fish, before it has caught sight of the angler or the reflected wave of his rod, is accurately and delicately made, and if the fly floats in its natural position without drag or curl in the gut, you will probably rise, and possibly kill, the most highly educated trout or grayling in the clearest water, while the slightest mistake will as probably set the fish down for the next half-hour. But much of this success depends on when this first cast is made. It may often pay you better to wait ten minutes before the first cast is made than to make it as soon as you are in position. A good fish is in this respect not unlike a stag; you may take hours to stalk him, and find him in such a position that a favourable shot is almost an impossibility. The practical sportsman will wait for an hour until the stag changes his position before using his rifle, and it is certainly far better to kill after waiting than wait after scaring. The same rule holds good with fish.

To put theory into practice, suppose the angler catches sight of a fish rising fairly well (selecting for

choice one under his own bank), the first problem is
to get within throwing distance without betraying
your presence. Starting at thirty yards below the
spot, and keeping well back, so as not to scare any
other fish on your journey, crouch down as low as
possible, and creep up, still in the crouching position,
until within about twelve yards of the place. If
your fly is not quite dry, you should dry it in the air
before approaching. When the wind is gusty creep
up during a cat's-paw, get into position, wait during
the succeeding calm, and cast when the next gust
ruffles the water. Let out line sufficient in your
judgment to cover the fish, and take the greatest
pains to make the first cast accurately, but, above
all, beware of waving your rod backwards and forwards in such a position that the flash of it on the
water is visible. This will infallibly leave you waiting in vain for the next rise of a fish that has pru-
dently beaten a retreat and departed to happier
hunting grounds. One more piece of advice. If all
your precautions and efforts fail to tempt the fish,
retire in the same crouching position, and do not
stand upright and expose yourself clearly defined
against the sky-line to the vision of the trout; even
if you are unable to come back to him later yourself
you may thus give the next passing fisherman a
chance, and nothing more surely indicates a thorough
sportsman than consideration for other anglers.

Example, they say, is better than precept. A
nobleman residing within a comparatively short dis-

tance of the metropolis had kindly granted me permission for a day in a small stream running through
his park, adding, however, the well-considered advice not to expect much sport, as the owners of a
number of gardens extending to the edge of the
water on the opposite side had always enjoyed—and,
it is to be feared, much abused—the privilege of
fishing and killing every trout they could get with
worm and minnow. Arriving on the scene of action
on an early June morning, I found the water pretty
and promising-looking, with trees of all sorts along
the banks, throwing out branches which met over the
stream. In the whole length of a mile there was
only one open place in which it was possible to fish
with the usual return immediately behind the angler.
To this spot the keeper took me at once. On cross-
examining him, it appeared that practically all his
lordship's friends patronised this spot, but that one
resident in the vicinity, who was generally most successful, never fished there, but, to use the keeper's
own expression, was "allers poking about among the
trees with a short rod and a partiklar fly of his own
tying." On a prospecting tour, I gradually worked
my way down to the very bottom of the water, determined to fish it up with a dry fly wherever a possible fish was rising. The stream was beautifully
clear, and flowed at a fair pace. The only flies
visible seemed to be iron blues, of which here and
there an occasional specimen was floating down, not
appreciated by the trout. At length one close to

the opposite bank was taken, then another, and then
a third. The fish rose immediately under the bough
of an alder overhanging not more than a foot above
the surface. The artificial on the cast was a star-
ling-winged hare's ear, the body ribbed with flat
gold; to my great delight, I succeeded at the first
attempt in putting it about a foot above the fish's
nose. In such a position a trout seldom sees a floating fly, except the natural duns, and hence it was
taken without the slightest suspicion. It being impossible to raise the rod into a perpendicular position,
it was some time before the first impetuous rush up-
stream of the hooked fish could be checked, but at
length the pressure of the rod, bent nearly double,
turned him, and eventually brought to the net a
good-looking trout of 1 lb. 6 oz. Continuing up-
stream, and trying every feeding trout under the
shade of the trees, each time the fly was accurately
placed the first throw, the result was invariably that
the fish rose at it, and was either killed, returned, or
lost, while on each occasion that the first cast was in
any way bungled the trout gave up rising. A considerable number of flies and strands of gut were left
in the boughs of the trees, and eventually, at two
o'clock, finding that my bag contained four brace of
as pretty trout as ever charmed the eyes of an angler
(weighing $11\frac{1}{2}$ lbs.), and having returned as many
more, I gave up fishing, although the trout were still
rising very well. During the whole time no fly except iron blues was seen, and yet every one of the

fish hooked or killed took the gold-ribbed hare's ear, which by no possible stretch of the imagination can be considered an imitation of the bluish-tinged wings and purple body of the iron blue.

Another illustration of the efficacy of the first cast occurred in September last with a party of three on a Hampshire stream. Our host, being desirous of trying the upper portion of his water until lunch-time, posted Mr. H. and myself at the lower end, which contains a very good stock of both trout and grayling, some being of great size. It was a sultry, oppressive day, with a southerly wind, and to one unaccustomed to these rivers the absence of movement on the surface of the water might have given the idea that there were very few fish. My friend H. had a fancy for a narrow piece about three hundred yards long, extending from a foot-bridge to a weir, in which were set a series of eel-traps, and leaving him there, I wandered aimlessly down to a taking-looking shallow at the bottom. Here I sat down, put my rod together, and laid it down with the cast in the water to soak the gut. Presently I saw a trout about 3 lbs. just under my eyes busily engaged in appeasing his appetite with that aggravating insect the *smut* or *fisherman's curse*. The bank being overgrown with sedges, I was invisible to him. After rising him short with three or four different patterns I pricked him, and put an end to my amusement. The previous day I had dressed some *red tags* with a bit of scarlet ibis instead of wool, and

with a desire of trying the improved pattern, knotted
one to my cast. Just where a cart-track crossed the
river in the widest part of the shallow a fish rose
several times at the pale watery-looking duns which
were hatching. I crawled up into position, and after
measuring the length of line by a preliminary flick
over the meadow, at the first cast the fly landed
right, and never having been wetted, of course
floated admirably. There was a quiet rise, and down-
stream the hooked fish went like a shot, and after a
good fight succumbed—a grayling, 2 lbs. 1 oz. Thinking it would be friendly to give H. the *tip* as to
the killing fly, I started to walk up, but before going
a hundred yards saw the head and shoulders of a
big fish out of water in the centre of a deep but
rather rapidly running horseshoe turn in the river.
Crouching down behind the bank, I waited another
rise to make sure of the exact spot, and at the first
cast again the fly was rightly placed, and the grayling (one of 2 lbs. 9 oz.) was landed after a grand rush.

Meanwhile H. could not get a single chance, but
at my request put up one of the red tags. But it
was of no avail. Each time he tried a fresh fish the
first cast did not come off accurately, and the fish
went down. Fly after fly and fish after fish were
thus tried in turn, but all to no purpose, as, although
a first-rate performer usually, he seemed on that day
to be out in his judgment respecting the first cast.
Ex uno disce omnes.

Many anglers will be disposed to urge that it is

a matter of comparative indifference to them as to *when* they throw to a rising fish, and that the only important point is *where* they throw, or, in other words, to place the fly accurately. No doubt they are, to a certain extent, right in their contention, and the question of accuracy and delicacy combined, especially in the first cast over a fish, is, as a general rule, by far the most essential object. Yet with very shy fish there is a right and a wrong moment to throw, and hence the subject is worthy of some consideration by all dry-fly fishermen who are desirous of following up the more scientific portion of the question. To a mere pot-hunter, whose only object is to kill as many fish as he can in a given time, it will not be an interesting study; his tactics are simply to keep on throwing over every feeding fish he can see from morning to night; and although he imagines he will get a larger bag, it is one of the many cases in which his very eagerness defeats itself, and certainly he does not derive the same satisfaction from the pastime as the less jealous and more unselfish fisherman who is worthy to be styled a sportsman.

With a trout poised close to the surface of the water, and merely opening his mouth slightly to suck in each passing fly, it is scarcely possible to be wrong; but when in such a position he is only taking one out of six or seven flies floating over him, the least splash, or sometimes even the mere gleam of the gut, will be enough to set him down, and the farther from the bank the position of the fish the more gut-shy he seems to be ; hence the axiom : " Never fish with duns one in mid-stream when you can find one rising under the bank." With a trout, the true secret under such conditions is not to be in too great a hurry to make your first cast, and not to throw too frequently. Cast a perfectly dry fly, cocked with greatest care and accuracy, twice, or at most thrice, and then rest the fish for three or four minutes, or at least until he has again risen at a natural ; then throw once or twice more. If this second attempt proves unavailing a study of the fly on the water is frequently useful, as a change to one merely a trifle lighter or darker, or a size smaller, may be found successful, although it is to a great degree doubtful whether the trout are so dreadfully particular as to a mere shade of colour. On the other hand, it must be admitted that a number of the same flies, hatching at the same time, are to our eyes identically alike in colour, form, and size.

Do not be too sure, having seen a good many of any particular fly on the water, that fish are taking that fly, as when a new species hatches out it may be sparsely distributed among the prevailing insects, and the fish may be selecting the last-hatched fly, which, if you are below, will account for your not seeing that fly floating past you in that particular run ; and fish, as a rule, take every fly on its first appearance in preference to one which has been up some time.

As an example, after the olive-dun has been up for

some weeks, the first appearance of the iron-blue should be persistently looked for, as very often, after the first day, fish will over and over again let the olive pass them, and take every iron-blue floating down.

A point which is intimately and inseparably connected with the question of when to throw is when not to throw; and with trout it should be remembered that they are more easily scared, and hence should be cast over less frequently and rested more often than grayling. A bad moment to select to cast over fish rising only moderately well is just after they have taken a natural fly, as they frequently go down with the fly in their mouths to *ruminate*, or possibly enjoy the flavour. A very shy fish, however, in still, smooth water, on a hot, calm day, can occasionally be tempted by a good imitation immediately after he has risen at the natural insect, or, as Ronalds puts it, by "casting into the ring of the rising fish." The disturbance he has himself caused by the act of rising seems to cover any little splash made by the cast, which under other circumstances would set him down. This plan is specially successful with smutting fish, as they usually come to the surface, and moving slowly along, suck in some six or seven of these aggravating little wretches, and then go down below to digest them.

As previously remarked, a trout rising in a small slack bay or eddy is a very difficult fish to tempt, owing to the artificial fly generally travelling down the stream, and being dragged by the line out-side, while the natural is almost stationary, or else drifts up with the eddy. In a place of this descrip-tion a fish takes duns or spinners, very much in the manner above described with *curses;* coming to the surface, and moving with barely perceptible motion just under water, he clears off every fly in the bay or eddy, and then goes down to await a fresh hatch. Should a sudden gust blow all the flies in the eddy off the water, the observant angler would often succeed in deluding the fish by placing the artificial just in the bay ; or sometimes even the fish will, when his stock of food in the eddy is thus exhausted, come outside or on the edge of the run, where the cast is a very simple one, and when the moment is propitious.

When fishing a slow-running stream, it is a sen-sible plan to leave your fly on the water as long as it will float. A very good illustration of the wisdom of this course occurred to my friend Marryat in my presence. It was during the later part of the May-fly, at Newton Stacey, when the fish were taking the spent gnat. In an almost stagnant bay of a small side stream a quiet rise had been seen. Across the neck of this bay a plank was extended to serve as a bridge when walking up the stream. Without a moment's hesitation, Mr. Marryat cast his spent gnat over the plank into this little bay, and waited for some minutes, when his patience was rewarded by a bold rise. The moment the fish was hooked, the keeper, at his request, slid the plank away, and the trout—a good one, nearly 3 lbs.— was dragged out into the stream and there killed. Not one in a hundred anglers would have waited so long for the rise, and the smallest movement of the rod would have produced a drag on the fly, and infallibly scared this wary old stager.

With grayling the question of when to cast is not so important as with trout. The former, when feeding on surface food, usually lie in mid-stream and deep down in the water, or even on the gravel at the bottom. Those curious lozenge-shaped eyes are designed for looking upwards, and from a depth of two and a half to three feet can distinguish the tiniest insect floating on the water. Grayling rise almost perpendicularly to the surface, and hence often *rise falsely*, or, in other words, miss the fly, either natural or artificial. When, however, they do secure it, they turn slowly over and go vertically down to their previous position, and in the motion of turning over often show their large dorsal fins and tails above water, thus making that unmistakable rise so well known to all in the habit of fishing for them. Practically speaking, the only moment not to throw to them is when they are thus going down head-foremost; and from their generally lying so much deeper in the water, they are less easily scared than trout, will stand being thrown over much more frequently, and require less resting.

Fish generally rise best at the commencement of

the hatch of a particular fly on any day, and this is accounted for in two ways first, because they, like other living things, are more hungry and keen at the commencement of their meal; secondly, because, although, as before said, it is questionable whether they are ever as particular to mere question of shade in the artificial fly as the fisherman is, they have not quite *got the colour* in the earliest portion of the hatch, and hence are not quite so critical as to the pattern of artificial as later on. There is, beyond doubt, however, much to be urged on this point, as every experienced fisherman will remember in his own case numerous instances of days when at the commencement of the rise he has killed a brace or two of fish with a fly at which they would not look later on. A further study of the natural insect having in such an instance enabled him to change for a better match of colour or size, he has found them come on the artificial again, and been again successful.

Another point worth noticing is, that it generally happens with a good hatch that the Ephemeridæ come down in droves of six or seven; then there is a small space or break, then another drove, followed by another break, and so on. In trying a fish taking nearly every fly of such a hatch the moment to cast can hardly be wrongly chosen; but when the fish are only taking moderately, it is a good plan to watch for the drove coming down, and throw a thoroughly cocked dry fly in the break, so that when floating down it heads the natural insects.

CHAPTER VI.

STUDIES OF FISH FEEDING.

A DRY-FLY fisherman requires at all times to keep his senses of hearing and sight at full tension, and to note systematically every circumstance or movement in the water likely to betray to him the *locale* of a feeding fish. This very state of tension is often likely to lead him astray, as straining every nerve to hear or see the rise makes him superlatively sensitive to the faintest sound or smallest disturbance on the surface of the water; and hence, in his excitement, he is often irresistibly impelled to waste his time in drying his fly and floating it over what, after all, does not turn out to be a rising fish—that is, one sucking in winged insects on the surface of the stream.

A *past master*, however, who has often spoilt a favourable day by this useless hunt after the impossible, will always make quite sure that the apparent rise to which he intends devoting his attention is a real one, and as a first point establishes to his own satisfaction that it is a fish, and not, as well may be, a rat sitting close to the edge in a bay out of sight and feeding on some of the various forms of vegetable food he affects, or a dabchick diving under water when scared by the angler's approach, and then just putting his beak above water a few yards higher up or down the stream to take a fresh breath, giving very much the appearance of a rise. If this apparent rise is seen twice or more times in succession in exactly the same place it is almost certain to be a fish, as the dabchick generally swims or dives either up or down, and repeats the apparent rise elsewhere. An obstruction, such as a floating stick carried to and kept against the bank by the current, or a bobbing rush only just reaching to the top of the water, or a curling eddy turning over stone, frequently produces very much the appearance of a rising fish.

Having determined that the movement is caused by a fish, it is far from certain that because that fish is making waves, or apparent rings or bubbles, he is rising at or feeding on surface food. He may be *bulging, tailing, smutting,* or *minnowing;* or the commotion may be brought about by two fish fighting. Of the symptoms indicating bulging, tailing, or smutting I will treat in a later portion of this chapter. When minnowing, trout usually make a quick dart through the water, and the fry are often seen leaping to escape their open jaws. When fighting, they generally rush headlong at each other several times in rapid succession, until the stronger has driven the weaker off his vantage-ground. It is well to note that, except when spawning, grayling very rarely indulge in pugilistic encounters.

Being certain that the movement in the water is that of a fish, and of a fish feeding on flies, the angler's next difficulty is to spot the rise, or to place its position. When under the bank this may generally be accomplished by fixing the eye on some striking object opposite to it, such as an extra high spear or a particularly bright patch of sedge, or a flower, or a brown hollow place in the ground, remembering, however, that the ring made by the rise must naturally drift down-stream, so that the rise is almost invariably placed below its actual position. I believe that this inaccuracy of judgment is increased owing to the sense of hearing usually giving the first warning to the angler; and in the space of time occupied by the sound travelling to the fisherman's ear, in addition to the moment which must elapse between hearing and seeing, the mark of the rise is carried some distance farther down than one would expect. When, however, the rise takes place in mid-stream it is far less easy to place it, as, in addition to the difficulties above referred to, the only guide to assist the angler in determining the precise spot is, generally speaking, the apparent distance and direction from some rough run or break on the surface, itself a changing and moving object.

Sometimes a rising fish is accurately marked down, and a good imitation of the natural fly on the water floated over him without result. The next rise of the same fish is three or four yards higher up, and the angler, in response to it, either crawls up or lengthens his line the required distance, and covers the last rise again with no result, and a few minutes later the fish is again seen taking a dun, having travelled three or four yards still higher up the stream. This wild-goose chase may, in some instances, be repeated time after time, until the trout has, by successive steps, moved as much as forty or even fifty yards. At length no more rises are seen, and the natural inference is, that the fish is set down. Looking back, however, to the place where the first movement of the fish was observed, he may be found steadily continuing his interrupted meal there in safety. Such a fish is a most tantalising one, usually of large dimensions, well fed, and in good condition ; very shy either of gut or the smallest mistake, and as often as not, has been hooked many times before, so as to be quite alive to the dangers of the position. If not hooked the first cast, the fisherman is advised to leave him altogether, and find a more unsuspecting prey elsewhere.

It is not an unusual occurrence to see a trout working slowly and gradually up-stream close under the bank, rising occasionally on his journey, and sucking in a fly here and there. If this is noticed, before making a cast wait patiently, and do not throw until he has settled down to feed in one place ; the fish is simply sauntering up to his habitual *salle à*

H

manger, whetting his appetite with a passing insect as a sort of *hors d'œuvre*, and will presently commence his dinner, taking his own particular seat at a favourite corner. When a fish has thus settled down to feed in a particular spot, it is said on the Test to be *in position*. I have observed that a fish will, at times, come up-stream a short distance to take each natural fly floating over him ; but more frequently drops slowly back tail first, with his nose close to the fluttering insect before either taking or refusing it, in either case returning to his original position. It is well to notice these little peculiarities, and place the fly accordingly either well above or comparatively close to the place where the fish is lying.

When looking up or down from any great distance, it is almost impossible to locate the rise exactly. Possibly taking a quick glance at the bank, noting some striking object apparently opposite to it, and at the same time measuring mentally the distance from the margin, may assist, but it is impossible under such circumstances to *spot the rise* accurately. The fisherman may be advised in such a case to crouch, keeping down, well away from the water's edge, and taking advantage of any shelter to keep out of the extended range of vision of the trout's sharp eyes ; to creep up until he has, as nearly as he can judge, got into position, and then wait patiently for a second rise. Natural impatience often impels an active-minded man to fish *on spec*, persuading himself that he has the place all right, and then he keeps on persistently flogging, in the hopes of tempting his quarry. One of two results will certainly ensue; either he keeps on throwing below the fish and tires himself by his useless exertion, or else his fly is placed too far above, in which case it usually drags; this sets the fish down for the next half-hour, besides adding a little more to his already advanced education.

Nothing is more aggravating to an enthusiastic angler than, after patiently casting for half an hour or more over a feeding trout or grayling, to find, when hooked, that it is a wretched little fingerling instead of the noble three-pounder his fancy painted it. In some cases it is impossible to form any estimate of the size of the fish from observation of the rise, but in other cases experience enables a fisherman to arrive at a fairly good estimate from the nature or position of the rise, the sound made, or other circumstances; and this power of estimating size is an important factor in the comparative success of a number of men fishing the same stream on the same day and under the same conditions. The most careful, the most experienced, and the most observing are, however, at times quite out in their judgment on this point.

In speaking of *rises*, it may be explained, in passing, that the expression is used to describe the act of a fish taking flies on the surface of the water, whether Ephemeridæ, either in the sub-imago or the imago state, winged Phryganidæ on the surface of the water, or flies hatched on land, such as the cow-dung, red ant, &c. A fish taking caddis, shrimp, or snails is said to be *tailing*, from its tail appearing at intervals above water, when the head is buried in the weeds; when feeding on larvæ or nymphæ it is described as *bulging*, from its motion through the water; and when taking "curses," or black midges or gnats, it is spoken of as *smutting*.

Probably the best means of judging size from the rise is derived from the sound produced by the act of breaking the surface when taking a fly, and the comparative weights may be said roughly to be arranged in a scale of harmony, the heaviest fish being the lowest bass, and smallest the highest treble; the intermediate notes indicating the intermediate sizes. In applying this test of sound, it must, however, be remembered that it is only applicable to the case of a fish remaining stationary and sucking in the fly passing over the spot where it is lying. The case of a fish following and dashing at a passing fly produces some confusion in the scale. The volume of sound is to a considerable extent dependent on the relative size of the insects themselves. A fish only just separates his lips sufficiently to enable him to take in the fly, and experience tends to show that the shyer the fish the less widely he opens his mouth, so that with a small insect the sound is comparatively faint, and with a larger one louder in proportion. A splashing rise in day-time is never a likely one,

and in the majority of instances is made when
taking larvæ or nymphæ, and not duns or spinners.

When rising frequently it may be fairly inferred
that the fish is well on the feed, and is likely to
take the artificial the first time it comes over him
accurately, floating and cocked. On the other
hand, having seen a trout rise only once, and
waited patiently for say five minutes, without
result, for a second rise, if the exact position has
been *spotted*, it is often well to throw carefully and
at longish intervals; and perhaps, after a dozen or
more ineffectual casts, at length the fish is tempted
and killed. A large trout often takes with a quiet
suck close under the bank, making a mere bubble
instead of the ring so generally looked for. This
bubble floating down is at times the first indication
to the fisherman of there being a feeding fish at
all; and in this case it is well to wait and watch
for a rise five or six yards above where the bubble
was seen, close to, in fact under, the overhanging
bank, or against a standing rush or bit of weed
or stick stranded against the very edge of the stream.
A rise of this description in very slow-running water
looks like the movement of a minnow, and is too
often passed as unworthy of notice by inexperienced
anglers; or if thrown to at all, a careless indifference is displayed in drying or placing the fly. At
such times the scaring, pricking, or hooking of
the fish is quite a revelation in the shape of a
heavy wave made by a trout of two or three

pounds when dashing away from the bank. No amount of care in drying the fly and placing it accurately and lightly in such a position is thrown away.

A trout jumping out of the water is certainly not rising; but what causes the fish to take these sudden leaps is more or less a matter of conjecture. Some of the modern authorities say that it is done by the Salmonidæ with the object of falling flat on the surface of the water, and stunning or killing a parasite with which their skin is at times infested. A quick rush through the water and a break of the surface is occasionally caused by pike or large trout chasing and striking at minnow, dace, or trout fry. This is, however, hardly likely to be taken for a rise by any but the merest tyro, the sound being unmistakable; and very frequently, too, the minnows or fry are seen leaping out of the water in their endeavours to elude the hungry jaws of their pursuer.

At times both trout and grayling will dart rapidly to the surface, take a fly, and as rapidly dart away again. This is an undoubted rise, but not a hopeful one for the fisherman, as it is either a very shy fish, not likely to forgive the slightest mistake or bungle, or, worse still, it is the case of a fish who, in the very act of taking the fly, has caught sight of the angler and beaten a headlong retreat. Sometimes a fish, rising steadily and slowly in mid-stream, will show his head above water, then his dorsal fin,

and at times even his adipose fin and tail.   In such
a case, try and see whether it is a trout or a grayling.
If a grayling, it is not unlikely that he will be
tempted.   The shape, colour, and size of the dorsal
fin will often enable the fisherman to make quite
sure of the species ; and on the rare occasions when
the tail is visible, the difference in shape between
the forked one of a grayling and the straight or
even slightly convex outline of a trout's tail is so
marked as to be easily distinguishable.   If, however, the fish making the head and tail rise is a
trout, it may be considered as a bad sign, and an
·indication that he is feeding on larvæ quite close to
the surface.

In deep, slow water a quick flip on the surface is
usually the rise of roach or dace, whose presence is
generally further indicated by a quick succession of
rises on the part of a number out of the shoal comparatively close together.   Many Hampshire fishermen are fond of selecting a fish just showing the
point of his nose above water when rising; but
although, as a general rule, this is a good sign,
yet occasionally trout bulging at larvæ give this
idea, especially when the angler is directly below
the fish, where the movement up-stream is not
distinctly visible ; hence it is well to make quite
sure that the fish is positively taking winged flies
off the water.

Large fish, as a general rule, rise slowly and take
the fly quietly, while small ones more often come

quickly to the surface and dash down again with
equal speed. A splashing rise at night is considered
by many a sure indication of a good fish feeding on
sedge or other large flies ; and although occasionally
this opinion is borne out by facts, it is not by any
means a safe one to follow invariably, as the largest
and best-conditioned fish are frequently found taking the adult Phryganidæ as quietly and with as
little commotion as when rising at the tiniest of
Ephemeridæ in the middle of the day ; and all of us
have, time after time, wasted the few and precious
moments during which this maddening rise lasts in
trying for splashing fish, and when successful in
killing any of them, finding that they were small
ones, or, if sizeable, an autopsy showing few, if
any, sedges, and a considerable number of shrimps,
snails, or other molluscs, and nymphæ of both Ephemeridæ and Phryganidæ. I remember one evening
at the end of May 1885, having a day with my
excellent friend " Red Spinner ; " the fish rose badly
during the day-time, but in the evening, just before
dusk, every trout and grayling in the river seemed
madly on the feed, splashing continually, and apparently taking sedge-flies in all directions. The
difficulty was, which fish to select, as the whole
surface of the stream seemed to be in a literal boil.
For some time we both tried, and tried in vain, fish
after fish and fly after fly, and at length I managed
to secure one trout of $2\frac{3}{4}$ lbs. with a large " artful
dodger." On arriving at our quarters I opened

this trout, wondering what the autopsy would show, and, *mirabile dictu*, found the undigested food to consist of three or four May-fly nymphæ, three large dark sedges, and at least thirty fresh-water snails in their shells. Possibly these molluscs are in the habit, of coming near the surface of the water in the hot summer evenings. In any case, it may lead others to note the contents of the stomachs of trout killed under such conditions, to see whether it was an exceptional circumstance, or whether one may take it for granted that, in the majority of instances, fish splashing noisily during their evening meal are partaking of this heterogeneous diet.

" I tell you, sir, the trout were rising all over the place, and although I tried every fly in my book, I could not find out what they were taking." Season after season we hear this formula repeated over and over again by tyros, or sometimes even by old anglers who have not taken the trouble to study the subject thoroughly. If discussed *à fond*, it is generally found that every fish in the stream has been feeding ravenously, ploughing the water in all directions while following the food, but scarcely ever being actually seen to take a dun floating on the surface. On such a day the *dilettante* usually returns with empty creel, deploring his ill fortune at being unable to discover the particular form and colour of fly the greedy trout were affecting. The more experienced, and probably more earnest, votary of the art has often, by continual and varied observations, proved

to his own satisfaction the futility of hoping to be
even moderately successful under these conditions.
He knows only too well that the apparent rises are
bulges, and that instead of sucking in the duns
when hatched, the fish are busily engaged in chasing
and securing the Ephemeridæ in the nymph state,
before they have emerged from the shuck.

At times the indications of this preference for the
fly in the immature state are unmistakable. The
feeding fish have taken up their positions on shallows,
usually over or immediately below " celery beds," and
are taking some small objects under water in a space
of a yard or more on either side of their stations,
darting rapidly backwards and forwards to the right
and to the left, and after each mouthful returning
to the posts they had originally occupied, their pre-
cipitate motion through the water causing these
continual disturbances of the surface, whence the
expression *bulging* is derived.

As a rule, they take under water, but at intervals a fish here and there will follow his prey
to the surface, and only succeed in catching it
at the very moment it emerges in the sub-imago
dress. Some readers may inquire why the dun in
the nympha state should not be imitated, and, as
remarked in a previous chapter, it is my opinion that
the difficulty does not lie in dressing an artificial
grub fairly resembling the dun nymph, but in im-
parting to that imitation the motion and direction
taken by the natural insect at that stage of its exist-

ence. Some authorities recommend the use of a large sunk fly when trying bulging fish, but personally I have never found this advice of any assistance, although, to a certain extent, one cause has ever operated against the chance of success, that being the fact that, not having confidence in the use of a large artificial when fish are feeding on a small natural, I have tried it in a half-hearted way, and without any faith in the experiment.

On rare occasions one hears of a brace or two of bulging trout or grayling having been killed by a comparative novice with wet-fly dragging, or even fished down-stream; and once or twice I have positively seen such a thing occur. Possibly these tactics might be adopted with advantage on private streams which are seldom fished, but on club or subscription waters, where the fish are highly educated, they are not likely to prove of much avail. One point, however, should be borne in mind, that, after all, a bulging fish is feeding and looking out for food, so that if by any chance he catches sight of a tempting morsel drifting past him, he is not unlikely to add this to previous items in his midday or evening meal. Hence, perhaps, a slightly showy pattern, such as an *orange bumble*, floated occasionally over the feeding fish, may be successful, but only occasionally, and by giving the trout or grayling a rest after each cast, so as to thoroughly restore his confidence, which may have been shaken by the gleam of the gut, or any little error of judgment in the preceding

throw. Probably, however, the very best fly to use
for bulging fish is the *gold-ribbed hare's ear*, and the
reason is not far to seek. Put side by side, under a
microscope with a low power (say a 3-in. or even
4-in. objective), a nymph of any of the Ephemeridæ
and an artificial of the above pattern. The most
casual observer will at once perceive that projecting
from each joint, excepting the last three, of the
abdomen of the nymph, there are fin-like appendages. These are called branchiæ, and are, in fact,
external prolongations of the respiratory organs used
for the purpose of extracting from the water the air
held in solution ; and the short hairs of the fur
picked out in the body of the artificial bear a very
strong resemblance to these branchiæ. If unable to
get a look from a bulging fish after a few attempts,
do not change your fly, but change your fish, and
then later on again, perhaps, return to your old love.
At times trout bulge at shrimp, snail, and caddis, as
well as larvæ and nymphæ, but more frequently when
feeding on them they are tailing.

It has been darkly rumoured that some anglers
are invariably able to get sport among bulging fish,
and that the plan adopted is to cast up-stream
with a good-sized sunk fly put directly above. The
slightest movement of the trout is answered by a
quick and somewhat violent strike, the effect of this
action being to drive the hook into some part of the
moving fish, but certainly not into his mouth. I am
inclined to doubt the possibility of accomplishing

this with a single hook, although it has been often vouched for by fishermen of ripe experience and unimpeachable veracity. Be this as it may, there is no word in the English language strong enough to express the utter contempt which a true sportsman should feel for a pot-hunter who would descend to such a strategy. It must utterly spoil a water, and for every fish killed at least ten must be pricked, scratched, or rendered shy, and any so-called fisherman detected in such an act should be "boycotted" by all true lovers of fly-fishing.

Sometimes fish, when feeding on larvæ and nymphæ, however, rise quietly, and do not move about much from place to place; and under these circumstances, it is almost impossible to distinguish the apparent from the *bonâ fide* rises, except by watching intently the surface of the water with the view of making certain that the winged duns floating on the stream are being taken. One such case is brought prominently to my mind, when on a hot August evening a trout rose steadily under the bank until it was almost pitch dark. For an hour or more I kept on throwing steadily, and, I am vain enough to think, without making any glaring mistake, over this fish. Commencing with a very small pale yellow dun (Flight's Fancy), then trying in succession a blue-winged olive, red quill, ginger quill, hackle-winged red spinner, Jenny spinner, and detached badger, I at length, as a last resource, put up a small silver sedge on a o hook. The very first cast secured a trout upwards of 2 lbs.; and knowing that fish feeding on *curses* will occasionally, for some occult reason, take this particular pattern, I fancied that I knew all about it, and made sure that it had been feeding on these annoying little insects. On my return home, an autopsy of the contents of its stomach revealed an extraordinary conglomeration of shrimps, caddis, snails, larvæ, and nymphæ, but not a single winged fly.

The expression *tailing*, as applied by the angler, refers to a fish lying with its head in the weeds gorging itself with shrimps, snails, caddis, young crayfish, or some of the many minute forms of animal life with which they abound. In order to force its head well into the thickest of the sub-aqueous vegetation, a series of vigorous strokes are every few moments given with the tail, which is, of course, at a much higher level in the water than the head—in fact, is as often above the surface as below. If carefully watched when feeding in this way in very shallow water every movement of the fish, from the tail to about the lower end of the dorsal fin, will be visible, the head and remainder of the body being hidden by the weeds, out of which it is actively engaged in extracting succulent morsels. First the tail rises, until half or more of it is out of the water; an energetic wag follows; the fish meanwhile turning half on his side, and boring his way down into the undergrowth, seizes all the food within his reach. This action sets a number of shrimps, larvæ of both Ephemeridæ and Perlidæ, &c., adrift, and as they float off from the weeds the fish's tail sinks, and his head as a natural sequence rises in the water, enabling him to secure a further supply to add to the mass already in his mouth. He then remains quiescent for a few minutes, probably while swallowing the mouthful, and then the operation of raising his tail and forcing his head into the weeds, followed by the depression of the tail and resumption of the horizontal position in the water, or rather near the bottom, is repeated *da capo*.

When, as usually happens, the tailing trout or grayling is in a deadish, shallow place, over thick weeds, the case is unmistakable; but when the depth of water above the weeds is a trifle greater, so that in the most vertical position the extreme tip of the tail only just breaks the surface, or does not quite reach it, and when, in addition to this, perhaps, it is nearly dusk, the appearance, especially if the fish, as large trout do, is moving slowly, is so similar to that of a rise that the most careful and observant anglers are frequently deceived. Not infrequently they keep on throwing over it time after time, even perhaps devoting some precious moments to a minute examination of the natural fly on the water, changing to the best imitation of that insect, and using the most anxious caution in approaching and casting with the greatest accuracy over what, after all, turns out to be the caudal appendage, and not the mouth, of the fish.

Various methods and diverse flies are recommended as likely to tempt tailing fish. Some say that a moderately large, flat-winged fly, such as an alder, governor, or caperer, fished wet down-stream, and dragging, will be found efficacious. Others, again, advise the use of a large showy grilse fly, well sunk, which should be thrown up-stream, well above the fish, and brought down quickly with two or three steady draws of six inches to a foot each.

To any one wishing to try this last plan, I would add that the cast should be made just as the fish's tail is sinking, so that the enormity called a grilse fly should be visible to the trout as his head rises in the water. It is obvious that, as long as the greater portion of the fish, including his eyes, is buried in the thicket of weeds, any object floating above that level cannot by any possibility be seen. Some anglers, especially the selfish ones, are in the habit of using a huge bunch of peacock herl for wings over a silver body, called the "Alexandra." What a profanation to bestow on this monstrosity the name of one of the most charming and amiable princesses of this century! It certainly is not the imitation of any indigenous insect known to entomologists; possibly the bright silver body moving through the river gives some idea of the gleam of a minnow. Long ere this its use should have been prohibited in every stream frequented by the *bonâ fide* fly-fisherman, as it is a dreadful scourge to any water, scratching and frightening an immense proportion of the trout which are tempted to follow it. It certainly *would* have been prohibited, too, but for the fact that experience shows that in any stream in which it has been much fished the trout soon become quite alive to its danger, and not only will not move an inch towards it, but when worked close to their noses will not so much as turn at it, but at times, on the contrary, even fly in terror from the dread apparition.

The best policy to adopt, perhaps, is to leave tailing fish alone. True, they are feeding, and feeding well; but they are ever intent on the shrimp, caddis, &c., drifting out of the weeds, or are partially submerged in the thickest of them with their heads down, and in a more or less perpendicular position; and no means are as yet known to the angler by which he can make his artificial lure travel in a similar way. A really good imitation of the fresh-water shrimp might at times be successful in basketing an odd trout here and there, and such an imitation has been dressed by my good friend Marryat, who has shown it to me. Both of us, however, have solemnly sworn never to reveal the secret of it; and as it is the only artificial fly of which we have ever demurred to give a pattern to any fisherman, and as neither of us ever uses it or even carries it in his book, this refusal must not be considered as a selfish action. In the heavily fished Hampshire streams it is surely desirable that the trout should be able to indulge in an occasional meal in safety with-

I

out being haunted by that dire dread and danger of the barbed hook? Honestly, I doubt if the artificial shrimp would under any circumstances prove killing; for, as in the case of the larva, it is at all events problematical whether the most natural imitation in colour, size, and shape would prove efficacious unless the active motion of the natural creature could by some means be imparted to it.

At times every trout on a shallow is tailing, and not a single rise can be distinguished, although possibly a considerable number of flies of different sorts and descriptions are floating down over them. To one residing permanently near a river, perhaps the best counsel in such case is to give it up in despair, and either go home or wait for a change of mood on the part of the fish; but to a busy man living in town, and only having rare opportunities of indulging in his favourite sport, this advice is too trying and disappointing. At all events, he must not expect much success; but if he must try, his best chance of getting a brace of fish with dry fly is to use a fancy pattern, such as the *orange bumble*, dressed on a largish hook, o long, which is not unlike one form of the shrimp; or at times the *furnace* will rise tailing fish when floated over them at the moment they are raising their heads towards the surface. Although the chance of killing tailing fish in a clear chalk-stream with a floating fly is very remote, and in the club waters, which are daily and hourly thrashed from end to end, practically *nil*, yet in private waters, where the appearance of an angler is a rarity, on a day when no rising fish are to be found, one of the above-mentioned flies may occasionally prove efficacious in picking up an odd fish; and in all such cases it must be remembered that the less the depth of the water the greater is the probability of the trout or grayling catching sight of the fly and taking it; and if tried at all, the very thinnest portions of a shallow over weeds should be selected in preference to the deeper channels flowing through the clean gravel.

On a still, hot, muggy day in July some two or three years ago, starting from the lower end of a favourite club water, I wandered in a somewhat disconsolate frame of mind gradually up the stream. Every now and again a fish would rise faintly and lazily to the surface, but the lightest and most accurate cast produced no response; and whether with smallest of flies on the smallest of hooks or larger ones; whether with sad and sober-coloured duns or gaudy fancy patterns; whether with winged flies or hackle ones or bumbles; whether floating, half-submerged, or even sunk; whether fished upstream, across, or down, the invariable result was nought. At length, reaching an eel-weir at the upper part of the water, and thoroughly exhausted by the long walk in waders and the high temperature combined, a smooth, sloping grassy bank tempted me to take a well-earned rest. Reclining well out of sight, and looking over the still, calm

surface of the stream above the weir, a gentle movement of a 3-lb. trout in the middle of the water
attracted my attention. It seemed to glide slowly
upwards, and scarcely making a ripple, just showed
the point of its nose above the water as it quietly
sucked in some tiny insect. It then gradually
dropped down until it was perhaps a foot below
the surface, and slowly swimming to the right, again
almost imperceptibly rose and took another fly;
then to the left, taking a third; then again it
leisurely sank to a short distance.

Four or five other trout were to be seen following
precisely the same tactics; and the water being as
clear as possible, the day perfectly calm, and the
light of that dead-grey, hazy type in which every
object in the water for many yards seems distinctly
visible, every movement could be discerned, and the
outline and even marking of every fish plainly
distinguished. This day was so pre-eminently a
typical one for smutting fish—or, in other words,
fish feeding on those microscopic black midges
usually called the *fisherman's curse* or *smut*—
that, though loth to intrude personal experience
on my readers, I cannot help citing it as an excellent example from every point of view, save and
except only that of killing fish. The heat, the haze,
the absence of wind, the peculiarly languid way in
which the trout seemed to swim about in the slow-
running water, apparently without aim or object,
every now and then sucking in a fly or two, all com-

bined, as a typical example of that aggravating form of rising described as smutting.

Perhaps the most annoying feature connected with this particular subject is, that in the Hampshire chalk-streams, on a day when the smuts are hatching in great numbers, the largest and best-conditioned fish are ever on the feed, and take not the slightest notice of the most tempting-looking natural duns floating down over their very noses ; at the same time they will travel yards to secure a wretched little midge scarcely visible to the naked eye. There must be some specially *piquante* or attractive flavour in the tiny insect, or possibly a sense of security from the knowledge acquired by ripe experience of the almost insurmountable difficulty to the fly-dresser in imitating so small a fly.

There are certainly several sorts of smuts, varying in size, colour, shape, and other details, and of these four, at least, are well known to the observant angler. It would certainly tend to advance our knowledge on the subject if some entomologist of experience would give their correct scientific names, and describe in detail their life-history and metamorphosis. At the present time it is not even known to fishermen for a certainty whether they are bred in the water and swim about in the larva stage, rising to the surface to assume the perfect or imago state, or whether they are bred on the land, and their presence on the water is a mere accident. Probably, from the great number on the water at all seasons, it may be inferred that they are in their early stages water larvæ; but it is not, with our present limited knowledge, safe to take even this for granted.

The first on the list of smuts, and earliest in date of hatching, has long legs and a small glossy black body; it is said to be carnivorous, and to have been seen preying on the bodies of dead duns. It hatches in the early spring, from the opening of the season until the warm weather first sets in; but the trout do not seem to care much for it. Possibly the plethora of Ephemeridæ in the larva and nymph stages, together with shrimps, young crayfish, and other crustacea, at this time of the year are more attractive. As soon as the weather becomes genial, and throughout the summer, the most prevalent smut has a short black body, the female being, as is the case with most insects, much larger than the male, and having distinct white tips to her wings; the male is, on the other hand, much smaller, and not unlike a diminutive edition of the hawthorn-fly, with clear wings. Another form of the *fisherman's curse*, having a clear tortoise-shell body, is frequently out in considerable numbers during the hot weather, and in the early autumn finds its way indoors, and is seen in rooms of houses adjoining the streams, covering the ceilings in great quantities. Later still in the autumn a smut looking like a very small horsefly is abundant. This has a dull bluish body, and is on the water even during the coldest winter days; in fact, in December 1885, during a hard frost after three o'clock in the afternoon, I saw a trout rising freely and taking every one that came over him.

As to the dressing of imitations of the smut, ooo hooks, being the smallest made, must, although far too large for the size of the natural fly, be invariably used. The tortoise-shell-bodied variety should be dressed with body made of a couple of strands of cock golden pheasant tail, legs of cock starling hackle, and wings of young starling very small and flat; in fact, all species of *curses* should be tied with the wings as flat as possible. For the more usual summer pattern, the body should be of black, shiny quill (that stripped from the central quill of the cock chaffinch tail being perhaps the best), cock starling hackle, and wings for the male of palest starling wing, and for the female of starling tail, which has a distinctly marked pale buff margin to the feather, thus imitating the pale tip of the natural wing. The most effective-looking wing, however, is made of a single piece of pike scale, prepared according to Mr. Macnee's patent process, cut to shape, and laid flat along the top of the hook. Another good rendering is Sir Maurice Duff-Gordon's, a black silk body, with silver tag, hackled with a badger hackle, worked over a couple of turns of black ostrich herl. These various dressings are given, although no angler must expect, unless under very exceptional circumstances, to make a bag with any of them. True, some years ago, Mr. H. S. Hall, at Dorchester, did kill two or three brace of good fish on a hot, bright day with the pike scale pattern, and he and others have on rare occasions repeated this success. When, however, one considers how heavily the fisherman is handicapped with such very small hooks, and the necessity for using the very finest of gut at a time when the weeds are in their most vigorous and luxuriant growth, it is not surprising that so large a proportion of rising fish are either scratched or not hooked at all, and even when fairly hooked, manage to break the hold of the diminutive barb, or inextricably entangle themselves in the dense vegetation.

Smutting fish, however, are undoubtedly fish rising and taking surface food, and are to be killed with floating flies ; but the best tactics to pursue are not to fish imitations of the smut, but to use certain flies which have been proved by experience to be effective under such conditions. Patterns to be used with success vary to a certain extent in different rivers or in different parts of the same river, and, of course, the more persistently a water is flogged the more shy and suspicious the fish become, and the more difficult to delude.

Why the fish should take these particular patterns is a complete mystery to all who take the trouble to think about the matter, especially as no one of them bears the smallest resemblance to the

natural fly in size, form, colour, or any other characteristic. As far as known to me, and for what it is
worth, the following, however, have proved in my
experience the most deadly artificials — viz., for
either trout or grayling, the Wickham; or, better
still, the landrail - winged variety of it, usually
known as the pink Wickham, dressed on oo hooks,
should be tried first as the most likely, to be followed by the silver sedge on oo hook, red quill on
oo hook, orange bumble, and furnace. The Sanctuary on a large hook, No. 1 or even No. 2, is more
often taken by smutting grayling than trout. For
grayling, however, when taking the natural "fisherman's curse," no fly yet dressed has borne comparison with the ordinary red tag, or, even better still,
the improved pattern of that fly invented by Mr.
Marryat, in which the tag is, as usual, of scarlet
ibis, the hackle a good blood - red one, and the
body made of a single strand of macaw tail, which
is a brilliant metallic blue on one side, and a
bright yellow on the other. When this strand is
rolled on to form the body, it has the appearance of
being a yellow ground with a fine blue rib running
up it. What object, animate or inanimate, hatched
in the water or bred in the air, it resembles is a
problem not easy of solution. One parting word of
advice. With smutting fish, above all, remember
the importance of "accuracy and delicacy combined in the first cast."

CHAPTER VII.

CIRCUMSTANCES AFFECTING THE ANGLER'S SPORT.

OF all circumstances most usually credited with exercising an influence, whether prejudicial or beneficial, over the angler's sport, the state of the weather is, according to the works of most authorities on the subject, the predominant one. Although it cannot be denied that the force of the wind, its direction, the state of the atmosphere, the presence of sun or cloud, rain, and the ever-varying effects of light are certainly to some extent conditions which must be reckoned with in estimating the probability of good or bad sport on any one day, yet they are not the all-important factors that many eminent angling authorities would lead us to believe. If this is true (and I hold it to be true) of wet-fly fishing, it is ten thousand times more so when treating of the dry-fly fisherman's art.

To find a rising fish is the first problem, and the fish cannot be expected to rise until the insects on which they feed are to be found floating on the surface of the stream. They very seldom rise well unless these insects are plentiful, and hence it may be safely argued that the most important factor in

determining the dry-fly fisherman's chance of success is the presence in considerable numbers of
the Ephemeridæ, Phryganidæ, and other flies in
the winged state. This is usually called by anglers
a good hatch of fly. The word *hatch* is a convenient one, and hence I have used it throughout
this book in the above sense; but it must be
understood that it is a misnomer. The true meaning of the expression *hatch* is the metamorphosis
from ova to larva, or in other words the change of
state effected by the larva first emerging from the
egg. This metamorphosis takes place certainly
with all Ephemeridæ and Phryganidæ at the
bottom of the river; and of all the water-bred flies
on which the fish habitually feed, the only one
which is certainly hatched on dry land is the Alder
(*Sialis lutaria*). As used by the angler, however,
the word *hatch*, if applied to duns, signifies the first
appearance on the surface of the sub-imago immediately after it has split open and struggled out of
the shuck or envelope forming the outer skin of
the nymph; when applied to spinners, it refers to
the falling on the water of the imago either while
laying its eggs or soon afterwards, when its only
duty, the work of reproduction, has been fulfilled;
when applied to the Phryganidæ, it refers either to
the change from nymph to imago in those species
which undergo this change on the surface of the
water, or to the subsequent visits to the water by the
imago probably for the purpose of laying the eggs.

Referring to the first of these, viz., the hatch of duns, it is surprising that so very little study or attention has been devoted to the subject either by entomologists or anglers, and especially that the latter, whose sport is so largely dependent on this point, should not have made some serious attempt to work out the conditions under which they may expect either a plentiful or a sparse supply of floating food for the fish. Nothing is likely to elucidate this question but continual observations made simultaneously in different streams and different parts of the same stream on definite and identical lines, carried on from season to season, and the results methodically arranged for careful examination and consideration. This question is well worthy of exhaustive study on the part of modern dry-fly fishermen. I have devoted some attention to the subject, and have from time to time started in my own mind various theories to account for the prevalence of Ephemeridæ in the sub-imago state on some days, and its comparative scarcity on others. At first I fancied the temperature of the air was a controlling influence. This theory, however, was very soon disproved. Then the idea occurred that the temperature of the water or the relative temperature of the air and water had something to do with it ; and to work out this theory I never failed during two years when at the river-side to take two or three times on each day simultaneous readings of two thermometers, one registering the temperature of the

water, and the other that of the air.   The only result of these experiments was to strengthen a theory
I had conceived, that whenever the air temperature
fell below that of the water the hatch of duns ceased.
I still believe that as a general rule this theory is
correct, although my belief in it was very seriously
shaken on the 3rd December 1886, when, on a fine
cold moonlight evening, with the temperature of the
air at 30°, and that of the water at 36°, dark olive
duns were hatching freely, the grayling taking them,
and my friend hooking fish after fish, only losing
them one after another owing to his line freezing to
the rings of his rod.   After this experience I aban-
doned this continual taking of temperatures as unlikely to lead to any practical results.   As before
said, however, the subject is one worthy of careful
consideration and study.

For some years past, throughout the early spring,
the inquiry as to sport, especially on the Hampshire
chalk-streams, has seemed invariably to invite such
answers as, "This cold wind quite prevents the fly
from hatching;" or, "The fish never take well in a
northerly wind;" or, again, "How is it possible to
do anything with the wind directly down-stream?"
Or you may hear from a veteran loud regrets as to
the deterioration of climate in the good old country,
and fervent prayers for a light southerly breeze.
When philosophically considered, what does all this
amount to?   Three distinct and separate hypotheses,
all of which are more or less erroneous—first, that

with north wind the fly does not hatch plentifully ;
second, that what does hatch is not freely taken ;
third, the difficulty of throwing up-stream in the
teeth of half a gale. In a previous chapter I have
tried to show how the difficulty of casting against the
wind can be overcome, and my present object is to
deal with the first two points.

As to the first point, a northerly wind in the
spring usually brings with it a high barometer and a
low thermometer, and if these two causes are sufficient to reduce the temperature of the water to a
point only two or three degrees above freezing, flies
of the Ephemeridæ family do not as a rule hatch in
any considerable quantity. Apparently, too, in such
weather the water seems extraordinarily clear, so that
every weed and patch of gravel, and every trout or
grayling lying or moving on them, are most distinctly
visible to an angler standing on a bank raised slightly
above the surface of the stream. It is, however, held
by many authorities that this seeming extra clearness
of the water is only apparent, being due to the dull
leaden colour of the sky and to the extreme density
of the atmosphere, and that it does not of itself
indicate that to the fish looking upwards objects are
abnormally magnified or more easily distinguished
than under ordinary circumstances.

The question of temperature fortunately is not a
matter of conjecture but of fact, which can be defi-
nitely determined by practical experiment. It will
be found that there are very few days in the spring

during which, between the hours of eleven in the forenoon and three in the afternoon, a thermometer plunged in the coldest of chalk-streams will register less than 40° Fahr. At this temperature the early duns, both olive and iron-blue, will hatch freely, and an angler neglecting occasionally to keep on throwing over rising fish will be enabled for himself to note the number of these delicate little insects floating down the stream, and will at the same time probably improve his chance of getting good sport, no mistake being so continually made by modern fishermen as that of casting in rapid succession time after time over a feeding fish, until sooner or later some slight mistake is certain to rouse his suspicions.

To quote from actual personal observation, let us take May 8, 1885. It was a day on which a fresh breeze from the north-west was blowing, and so cold was it that, to an idler on the river-bank, it was a difficult matter to keep his hands warm; and yet the number of flies hatching was, even to one accustomed to the plentiful supply on chalk-streams, something astonishing. The trout seemed to have appetites which could not be appeased, rushing about in all directions, making heavy bulges under water as they took the larvæ rising from the bed of the river, or here and there just breaking the surface as they seized the fly at the very instant of its casting off the envelope in which it had passed the pupa state. This should of itself indicate the fact that it was a most unsuccessful day, and that the trout could not be persuaded to look at any artificial fly, as their every movement was to secure the swiftly darting larvæ when rising to the surface and before emerging from the *shuck*.

No doubt this particular failing of feeding on the imperfect grub is one that seems to increase from year to year, and for the dry-fly fisherman it is a most unfortunate one. To dress an artificial representing the larva or pupa is difficult, but not an absolutely impossible task. Having overcome his natural repugnance to descend from what may be described as *high art* to the less scientific sunk-fly style of fishing, and having succeeded in turning out a fairly good imitation, the amateur is prone to imagine that he has at last solved the problem, and can, by fishing it under water, make sure of a respectable bag at a time when the fish are bulging incessantly at the natural larvæ. Alas! how woefully he is *désillusionné*. The fish will not look at this, although it is an admirable representation, both in colour and shape, of the natural insect. And what is the reason? To elucidate this, take a handful of weed from the bed of the river, and extract from it three or four specimens of the dun larvæ with which it abounds; place these in a tumbler of clear water, and patiently watch. Those that are nearly ready to hatch, or are rising to the surface for that purpose, seem positively electrified, every feeler or leg, and every fold or rib of their bodies, moving in an eccentric but continual motion. How is it to be expected that a timid, shy fish like a trout, who from painful daily, and even hourly, experience is warned to use the keenest of all the senses with which he has been endowed by nature, viz., his sight, for his protection, should mistake that motionless supine compound of dubbing, silk, quill, and hackle drifting helplessly and lifelessly like a log down the stream, for the active, ever-moving larva sparkling in the sunshine, and varying in colour at every motion as rays of light strike it at different angles?

As to the second erroneous hypothesis, viz., that the fly when hatched is not taken freely during a prevalence of northerly winds. When the wind is down-stream the fish rarely have a fly put to them right, and hence appear to be less suspicious than when the wind is more favourable. North wind is generally a cold wind; a cold wind is an iron blue wind; the iron blue is the favourite fly of the fish in chalk-streams. Carry your memory back, or (if you are sufficiently methodical to keep a diary) refresh it by a reference thereto, and see how on the 18th of April 1885, a bitterly cold day, with a strong wind from that unpleasant quarter, the fish rose well from ten or eleven o'clock until four; how every fisherman on the water secured more or less sport; how your own bag contained two or three brace of really good trout, through your fortunately remembering and starting sufficiently early in the morning to secure that little bend or corner where the north wind was favourable; and how, when returning to your homely quarters,

K

tired and stiff from the unaccustomed exertion, and
your shoulder aching from the pressure of the strap
of your creel weighed down by a goodly load, it just
dawned on you that after all fish do sometimes rise
well in a down-stream wind, and when they do so
they take hold of the fly in right earnest, so that a
fair proportion of hooked fish are landed.   Contrast
this with the 21st of April, only three days later,
when your first glance out of doors showed you a
dull, leaden-coloured sky, with heavy banks of drifting clouds travelling quickly before a southerly gale.
Remember how the usually smooth portions of the
river were lashed into heavy crested waves by the
force of the wind blowing directly against the force
of the current.   You then wandered for miles, watching in vain for either fly or the welcome ring of rising
fish, and returned at night weary and disheartened,
with an empty basket, to find every one of your
confrères in an equally dismal plight.   The further
this reference to your diary or other reliable data
is carried the more you will be inclined to doubt
whether in the chalk-streams running from north
to south the time-honoured condemnation of a
northerly wind is not a worn-out and erroneous
impression handed down from generation to generation.   A southerly wind, which in these streams
blows directly from the sea, is usually a cold, damp,
and unpleasant one, bringing with it alternate squalls
and heavy rain.   During the showers the dry-fly
fisherman's muscles are fearfully overtaxed by his

efforts to keep the fly free from moisture, and in the intervals between the showers the rough up-stream wind is continually blowing the natural fly over and over in strange and unnatural motions, or forcing it upwards against the stream ; and wherever the fish are shy they will not rise freely at a fly behaving itself in this curious fashion, but seek their food in comparative safety at some considerable depth below the surface.

Yet on the very next day during which "rude Boreas" has been running riot, each and every one of you, when comparing notes in the modest village inn over your post-prandial tobacco, will revile your atrociously bad luck in getting such weather, and that delightful old colonel in the corner will again treat you to his special grumble on the dire effects of the Yankee predictions, or the School Board, or some other new-fangled and even *Radical* notion (pray pardon the word—no politics) on the climate of our well-beloved fatherland, and tell you how in olden times, during the "forties," the weather in spring was invariably a compound of warm, re-freshing showers, delicious, bracing, light southerly breezes, and long spells of beauteous sunshine, and how it is only since the advent of the transatlantic cables that these dreadful north winds have been introduced to damp, or rather freeze, our ardour. Do you think he really believes in the terrible theory he is advancing? Do you honestly think that the prevailing wind and weather during succes-

sive seasons have not as nearly as possible followed
the same immutable law of average ; and, above all,
do you think that the same beneficent Providence
does not now, as much as heretofore, adhere to the
eternal fitness of things, and send in due season heat
and cold, frost and rain ?

In southern streams the east wind is not, as a rule,
a favourable one ; it seems to be almost invariably
accompanied by haze, and in hazy weather the duns
do not appear to hatch freely. At the same time,
however, it sometimes happens that with east winds a
fair hatch of fly is seen, and the fish take well.   But
this must be considered exceptional.   Light winds
are certainly preferable to heavy ones.   Just sufficient wind to cause a slight ripple on the surface of
the water is the beau-ideal as to force ; less than this
makes it difficult to approach the water without
scaring the fish, and more than this makes it difficult
either to spot the rise, or, what is perhaps nearly as
important, to see your own fly when floating down
over the rising fish.   When the wind is very strong
and the surface of the water lashed into heavy waves
fish do not ever rise well.   The reasons for this are
not difficult to find ; the natural fly is whirled over
and over, and at the moment the fish thinks he is
just on the point of securing it, is as likely as not
suddenly blown off the surface of the water.   After
a few of these unsuccessful attempts he thinks it far
less troublesome, and a far more efficacious method
of appeasing his appetite to sink gracefully into the

depths of the weed, and there continue feeding on the shrimps, snails, larvæ, or caddis, whose movements through the water are not affected by the ·sudden gusts of wind. Grayling are even less inclined to feed on the surface in tempestuous weather; in fact, they seem generally more affected by change of weather than trout. Of course any fish taking well during a gale of wind are far more easily approached, will stand coarser gut, will take larger flies, especially when floating and cocked, and generally are more easy to get on terms with than in calm weather.

It is a preconceived notion among angling authors, and even among entomologists, that the Ephemeridæ do not hatch freely in northerly, easterly, or north-easterly winds ; and Pictet, whose work on this family is not only of the very highest literary character, but bears on every page the unmistakable impress of careful and truthful examination, states from his own observation in his own words, " Elles naissent peu lorsque règne le vent du nord." My own experience of the Test, and especially of the part of it fished by the Houghton Club, most distinctly contradicts this assertion, and I think I may say without exaggeration that every abnormally large hatch of the smaller Ephemeridæ witnessed by me has occurred on days when the wind has been northerly or north-easterly. The Test may be an exception to the general rule, but it would be well for anglers on other chalk-streams, or, in fact, on

any other rivers, to make observations, and record
their results in full, with a view of checking this
experience.

Bright sun in calm weather is, as a rule, fatal
to success; this is probably due to gut being very
visible in the strong light. Sometimes, however,
even on a bright, hot, calm day, there is a chance of
killing if the angler will take the risk of losing
an extra large proportion of his fish and use the
smallest of flies on the finest of gossamer gut.
In sunny weather fish seem wonderfully *gut shy*,
and perhaps it may be asserted without fear of contradiction that gut shyness is the prevailing form
of shyness from which trout and grayling suffer in
streams where they are frequently cast over.

During and after rain the fish, as a general rule,
rise well. For some two or three days beforehand,
however, they appear to be waiting for it, and either
do not rise at all, or if they do, indulge in an occasional peculiar *corky* sort of rise, certainly not taking
any fly on the surface, but coming up as if for air,
and almost immediately turning over and diving
down again. The moment the rain commences to
fall the fish commence rising, and although during
the rain it is beyond doubt difficult and hard work
to dry the fly, it is equally beyond doubt worth the
exertion if the angler is really desirous of getting
good sport, as nothing is so deadly as a perfectly
dry fly floating cocked over a rising fish in wet
weather.

And here I am about to embark on the most difficult part, not only of this particular chapter, but of the
whole subject; and yet it is, to my mind, so important
and so little understood by my brother anglers, and
so difficult to express intelligibly, that I feel almost
constrained to ask forgiveness beforehand if my
meaning is not quite clear.   Among Scotch gillies
it is not unusual to hear the expression, "The light's
no good," used to prepare the fisherman for a day
of despair and disappointment.   What does he mean
by this description which is best expressed in
English by the words "a bad light?"   A peculiar
state of the atmosphere intuitively tells him what
from his own experience he has had many opportunities of verifying, viz., that the fish will not take;
and without being able to offer any reason beyond
mere conjecture, I can confirm the truth of his pre-
diction, whether in a Scotch river or loch, whether
in a Hampshire chalk-stream or a turbulent moun-
tain brook, whether fishing in heavy pools for thirty-
pound salmon or whipping for three-ounce Devonshire trout.   It would not surprise me to hear that
even when bottom-fishing for roach or barbel, pater-
nostering for perch, spinning for pike, or even
bobbing for eels the same atmospheric conditions
would produce the same result, and that in this "bad
light" all forms of fishing alike were unsuccessful.

Now what is a *bad light?*   It is when the entire
hemisphere of the sky is of one heavy, grey, dull
leaden colour; when the very light itself seems to

have become imbued with this sad leaden tinge;
when the water appears unnaturally clear, probably
from its contrast with the dull grey tint of all
its surroundings; when every object in the water,
whether trout or grayling, whether banks of green
weed or patches of light clean gravel between the
weeds, are distinctly visible from an extreme distance.   Such a day in early spring is cold, and in
summer or autumn is oppressive, sultry, and pro-
ductive of headache and other *malaise* in human
beings; and on such a day I have never seen a good
hatch of duns, nor do I ever remember on such a
day good sport to have fallen to my lot or to that
of any other angler's on the same stream.   Probably
such a day is almost invariably the precursor of a
change of weather, and fish seem always to go off
the feed at the first signs of such a change, and wait
until the change has taken place before coming on
the feed again.   Thus, too, after a sudden rise or fall
of the barometer both trout and grayling seem for, a
day or two positively *glued* to the bottom of the
river until the result of the warning barometric
movement has developed.

On days when small fleecy clouds are drifting in
the sky, when the light is variable and the wind
changeable, when one moment the surface of the
stream is calm and lighted up by brilliant sunshine,
and the next moment a little puff of wind ripples
the water and the bright sunlight is dimmed by the
shadows of the morning clouds, frequently good sport

may be anticipated. On such days, however, it is well to remember that the fisherman should crawl into position during a gust of wind, wait during the succeeding spell of sunshine, and cast to his fish during the next puff. This advice has been given before in this book, but it is one of the golden rules to be observed by every dry-fly fisherman who wishes his efforts to be rewarded by success, and I will not, therefore, apologise for its reiteration.

It is said that thunder has the effect of putting the fish off the feed, and this assertion is correct to the extent that when the sky is obscured by heavy thunderclouds rolling and piling themselves up in preparation for the great *dénouement* there never is anything approaching a good rise. When the air is heavy, hot, and oppressive, when the thunderclouds are tinged with red and the sky here and there has a lurid appearance, when flashes of lightning are seen over the distant hills and the ominous roll of thunder indicates that every moment the storm is approaching, still not a rise is seen to break the still surface of the water. At length the storm breaks, vivid flashes of lightning overhead are followed almost instantaneously by heavy claps of thunder, and the rain pours down in a torrent. During the very heaviest of the rain the fish generally rise well, and although not a pleasant time to fish, yet it is, as a rule, worth the fisherman's while to brave the elements and persevere.

With uniform grey cloud overhead and occasional

light showers during the spring, fish generally take
well on a moderately mild day, and very often, too,
when it is raining lightly throughout the day. If
only the exertion of keeping the fly thoroughly dry
is undergone, the best of sport can be had; in fact,
in some parts of the Test and other chalk-streams
it has become almost a cant expression that the
fish are always *silly* in rainy weather. A bright
blue sky, with heavy white banks of cloud on the
horizon, even if there is not much wind and the
clouds are almost stationary, does not indicate a
promising day. It is always well to fish into the
sun, and hence avoid the angler's shadow being
thrown on the water; and as the sun gets lower
in the horizon, the shadows are naturally thrown
farther on the river, so that in the evening it is
most important to be on the eastern bank if possible. It is, of course, always well to fish up-stream
into the wind rather than down-stream with the wind,
although the work is a little harder.

It would be quite possible for anglers to compile
a very valuable set of data as to the days on which
they have been successful or unsuccessful, but to do
so it would be necessary for a considerable number
to collect and tabulate identical information on the
same days in different places; and the efforts of the
Manchester anglers to induce their members to
keep diaries and record any circumstance they deem
worthy of note, besides certain information as to the
state of wind, weather, barometer, thermometer, the

different species of flies hatching, &c., &c., &c., are most useful, well directed, and will, I trust, be crowned by success. A useful adjunct to every angler's diary would be what is called the *Beaufort Scale*, giving to each letter of the alphabet a distinct signification of some particular state of the weather, and which is, or certainly was, in use in the reports issued from the meteorological office.

On some days fish after fish apparently rise fairly at the fly, and the natural expectation of the angler is, at any rate, to hook a fair proportion, even if he is not successful in landing them afterwards. But no! On such a day time after time he strikes seemingly at the right moment, and with just sufficient force to drive the barb home, and either has a short run or a turn or two, and away comes the hook; or else he experiences no resistance to the action of striking, indicating that he has not even pricked the fish. A number of men on the same day, at the same or contiguous waters, compare notes in the evening, and find that the experience of one has been the experience of all, with the slight difference caused by the various degrees of shyness of fish in diverse portions of the same stream, due to having been more or less frequently cast over. This unfortunate propensity of rising at the fly, and either not taking it at all or else handling it (or rather mouthing it) so gingerly as to be insecurely hooked, is technically called among dry-fly fishermen *coming short*.

Before considering the various causes and methods

of *coming short* it will be well to clear away certain delusions indulged in on the subject. How often one hears it said, " Confound the fish; I keep on missing them to-day." This is quite a mistake. Once in a way a fish is missed through the fisherman's wits having for the moment strayed from the object on which he should be intent, and caused him to neglect raising his hand or striking at the rise ; but these cases are very few and far between, and even when they do occur the pluck of the fish is usually distinctly felt. It is not that the fisherman has missed the fish, but that the fish, either by a miscalculation of the speed of the current or of *malice prepense* has failed to take hold of the bunch of feathers and hook which we believe represents more or less accurately the natural insect.

On the other hand, it is not safe to infer that whenever a fish gets away through being lightly hooked it is due to coming short, as occasionally the fault is in the fisherman himself striking too quickly, sometimes even before the fish has taken hold of the fly, and the cause of this mistake is usually to be attributed to nervousness. It is well to note that striking either too soon or too late is, like many other bad habits, when once acquired, difficult to correct, and the most phlegmatic and coolest of men are to bo excused if they are more or less flustered at the rise of a big fish. Besides, to the angler himself it is so difficult to determine whether the strike was premature or the opposite, and a bystander is not always able to speak with certainty on such a point.   If the action of striking has been too violent, the discovery of the fact that the fly has been left in the fish's mouth is usually conclusive evidence.

Coming short is an indication either of the fish taking badly on a particular day or of their being very shy, or of a combination of these two disagreeable vagaries.   Accuracy and delicacy combined in the first cast over a rising fish will generally obviate this; at times, too, the use of very small flies will be found efficacious.   Thus it will often happen that on one of these disappointing days, using a fly on a o hook, rising fish, one after another, come short; but on changing to an artificial of the same pattern on a oo or even ooo hook the fish will be found to fasten, although the use of so small a hook as a ooo certainly does handicap the angler very heavily, and cause him frequently to fail to hook the fish.   It must, however, be remembered that when once the barb is fairly home the hold of the smallest hook is as secure as that of the largest, and the former undoubtedly is not so apt to cut out as the latter.

A slow rise is generally an indication of taking well, and, further, may, in the majority of instances, be considered a sign of a large fish, and in the case of a slow rise or large fish the advice cannot be too strenuously given not to hurry in striking.   On the other hand, a quick rise is usually made by a small fish or a very shy one, and should be struck quickly; in fact, to use a lawn tennis term, half-volleyed.

Large fish take a fly leisurely and reject it slowly, while small fish, as a rule, snap at it, and spit it out almost as soon as they touch it, especially grayling, and more particularly in north country streams, where they run small.

Another very prevalent form of coming short, especially in waters that are heavily flogged, is when a fish, rising steadily to all appearances, comes up to and takes the artificial fly fairly and well in the mouth, and the strike either just scratches or does not touch him at all. The only feasible way of accounting for this is, that the fish is highly educated, and hence very shy of the gleam of gut. He sees the fly, and starts with the intention of seizing it; when close to it he catches a glimpse of the gut, or there is some other circumstance which arouses his suspicion; but having given with his tail the necessary impulse to reach the surface, this arousing of his suspicions takes place at a moment too late for him to be able to check himself and refuse the fly. If able to do so, he then turns short either to the right or the left, and in the act of breaking the surface drowns the fly; but never having really taken it into his mouth, no action of striking can by any possibility hook him. Sometimes, however, he does not discover or suspect the danger until it is too late to turn to one side, when I firmly believe that a very shy fish simply closes his mouth and allows the momentum he has acquired to carry him to the fly, which he touches, and of course sinks it as he goes down. The effect of striking in this case is either to miss him altogether, or at least to hook him outside ; and after losing a fish in this way a single very small scale is often found firmly fixed on the barb of the hook. A confirmation of this theory is found, too, in the fact that these very small scales are only found on the back of the neck immediately behind the head. I remember one evening hooking a trout of about 3 lbs. who rose very much in this way. I could really do nothing with him for a time, and quite imagined he was hooked in the tail or one of his fins. On landing him, however, the hook, a oo, was found deeply imbedded in his snout, fairly between the nostrils, and it would appear impossible that a fish taking the fly fairly in his mouth could be hooked in this remarkable position.

Grayling are far more confirmed offenders than trout in respect to coming short, and, strange to say, it frequently happens that even when rising at the natural fly they fail to secure it. This, however, is probably due to their remaining at a lower level when feeding and coming up almost perpendicularly at a fly to take it, which very likely makes it a diffi-cult matter to calculate the exact angle at which they must rise to reach the precise spot to which the insect has been carried by the force of the stream, and thus accounts for their coming short so often. Whether they have caught or missed the fly, they almost invariably descend in a vertical direction to the same depth and the same position as they occupied previously. Another, and to my mind inexplicable peculiarity of grayling is, that for hours together every rising fish will come short, and very possibly not a single one will be landed. Suddenly, without any variation of weather or any other apparent cause to account for the singular change, every one will fasten, and the basket be filled in a comparatively short space of time.

In bright sun and clear water fish are very apt to come short, thus giving, if required, another proof of this provoking incident being due to excessive shyness. A fish coming any distance to secure a fly, either natural or artificial, is usually an indication of feeding well, but sometimes a trout will drop, tail first, down-stream for yards with his nose almost touching the fly, and after all refuse it, and return to his position in a most annoying way; this, again, is probably a case of extreme shyness, or of his suspicions having been aroused by some abnormal circumstance. In these cases he has generally satisfied himself that the particular pattern is a fraud. He will repeat the operation with a change of fly, and sometimes fasten after a dozen changes. The angler may go on casting at such a fish, remembering, however, not to put the same fly over him more than twice or at most thrice in succession.

On a certain part of the Test, a private piece of water, and one of the very best on the stream, which is certainly not overdone with anglers, both Marryat and I have found that the fish continually came unhooked in a mysterious manner, so much so that we gave to this particular style of losing the trout the name of the charming estate.

Rising fairly, and generally slowly, at the fly, and seemingly taking it well, the fish, when struck, goes off with a rush, and you congratulate yourself on being *well into him ;* and just as you begin to hold him hard the hook comes away. If this happened once, or even twice, it would provoke no special comment; but when, as I can positively aver from my own experience, it has occurred as many as twenty times in one day, the only inference is, that it is one more form of coming short; and a further evidence of this contention is found in the fact that an examination of the hooks often reveals the presence of a very small scale firmly fixed on the barb, which must be a conclusive proof of the fish having been hooked outside.

L

CHAPTER VIII.

SELECTION OF FLY.

ANY advice as to the pattern of fly to use under particular circumstances is easy, perhaps, to give, but it will, in all probability, not be usually followed by the angler. To begin with, every fisherman of experience has, with more or less good reason, his own fancies, and if he is using one of them will persevere for hours. If the fish take, this is another argument for the particular dressing, and if not he can always find an excuse to account for the want of success; either it was not dry enough, or not cocked, or did not come over the fish quite accurately, or the trout was set down by his first cast; in fact, the possible excuses are infinite in number. On the other hand, when the angler is using a pattern which he is not inclined to swear by, a very moderately dry fly placed somewhere in the vicinity of the rise in a somewhat careless way is sufficient to enable him to declare that, as he had predicted, it is the wrong fly, and hence he must change it to one of his pet patterns. My object in this chapter is not to advance the claims of any fly-dressers or of their inventions, or, to be more accurate, perhaps their imperfect copies of the beautiful works of nature (and, after all, the best of artificial flies are only very imperfect copies), but to do the best in my power to give the angling fraternity the benefit of any experience I have been able to gain during many years of dry-fly fishing in various rivers. Fortunately I am able to be more precise in these matters than many of the brethren, and to base my advice on the solid foundation of facts, having carefully kept a diary of each day's fishing for some ten seasons, and recorded in every case not only the fly with which each fish was killed, but also some particulars of the natural ones on the water, the state of weather, and other useful details.

Of course my data are mainly derived from club or subscription waters, in which the education of the fish has reached a very high standard, and where day by day, from the opening to the closing of the season, flies, dry and wet, floating and sunk, are cast with more or less precision over every fish, who, from bitter experience, must perforce get some idea of the dangers lurking behind the seemingly toothsome insect. I have not had many opportunities of trying the more favoured localities where the visit of the fly-fisherman is of rare occurrence, and the flashing of the glittering gut an unusual circumstance; but where I have done so, the conclusion arrived at has been that the selection of fly is of far less importance, and the accuracy and delicacy of far greater importance; that the detail of dressing the fly does not

require so much study, but that to keep out of the
keen range of vision of the trout, whether it be the
angler or his flashing rod, requires far deeper and
more careful study. In fact, it appears that the
effect of education on the fish, or, in other words,
the continual presence of fishermen plying their art
over them, is to make them far more suspicious
of the artificial fly or of any little mistake, and far
more shy of gut, but far more tolerant of the presence of man and the gleam of his accompanying
rod.

I purpose dividing this chapter into three sections—firstly, selection of fly for spring; secondly,
selection of fly for summer, in which I propose including the green drake or May-fly, and incorporat-
ing with it something of the life-history of the
natural insect, as well as hints as to how it should
be fished; and, thirdly, selection of fly for autumn
and winter.

SPRING.

The trout-fishing season commences in some portions of the United Kingdom as early, I regret to
say, as the 2nd of February, but the Hampshire rule
has, I think, been never to open before the 25th of
March; and even this date is, to my notion, certainly too soon. In what condition the Devonshire
trout may be in the early days of February I have
nothing but hearsay to guide me, but a Test fish

at the end of March, if more than say a pound and a half, is probably very far removed from what would be considered by experienced fishermen on the spot to be anything like good condition. I am convinced that if in the Hampshire streams the fish were allowed to feed in safety until the middle of April, say the 15th, the angler's sport would in the end improve, not only from the superior condition of the fish, but from the fact of their having become accustomed to take the flies floating on the surface without danger. But I fear that no argument of mine will avail much to induce the keen angler to abstain until so late a date; and, candidly, after a long winter my own sympathies are to a great extent with him.

As to selection of fly, say from the beginning of April, one must not be very far wrong, in the first selection, if it is intended to get a fair day's sport, as the rise is generally a very short one, — on a moderate day from twelve o'clock till two, or after a frosty morning following a cold night, the rise as a rule will not commence before one to half-past; so that within these small limits there is not a great deal of time for experiment. Sometimes, if the weather is mild, the fish will commence feeding only moderately well at a comparatively early hour —say eleven o'clock—and go on to four, or even five. Generally on such a day the rise is not fast and furious, but one can see a fish here and there taking; and especially if light and warm, but not heavy, rain

is falling it is usually a successful one. Yet at
times all these calculations are upset. The day is
one which would be considered absolutely made to
pattern. One goes out full of hopes, but from morning till night not a single rising fish is seen.
Perhaps one of the greatest charms of fishing is
this extreme state of doubt as to what one is likely
to achieve. However, for the early part of April,
the best patterns are some of the darker olives, such
as the rough olive, the india-rubber bodied olive, or
the dark olive quill, or for a change a blue quill.
When we reach the middle of the month the gold-
ribbed hare's ear is perhaps the most successful
of all, especially with bulging fish. This point has
been already treated in detail in a previous chapter.
If not taken well, and a change is thought desirable, the medium olive quill, a detached olive, or
a drake's extractor for olives; or, when they are
hatching, one of the various patterns of iron blues,
a fly which is far too often neglected by the south-
country fisherman, may be put up. In fact, it is
very questionable whether any dun is so well taken
when it is on the water as a really good imitation
of this particular species.

Almost the first mild days after the middle of
April will, in rivers where it is found at all, bring
the first signs of the grannom. There are so many
fallacies existing in the minds of even the highest
authorities as to this fly, that I am constrained to
criticise their dicta adversely. First of all they say

the grannom is essentially a fine-weather fly. Now
this is true as far as regards the old flies going
out to lay their eggs on the water, these being flies
which had changed from the nymph state some
days previously, and have become very much darker
in colour than when first hatched. They are usually
seen flying in great clouds through the air; they
occasionally dip and just touch the surface of the
water with the tail end of the abdomen, which is
probably the act of laying the eggs. Not one of
them is seen on the water, and naturally not a
single trout is taking them.

Then again we are told that at the first shower
of rain not a grannom is seen. This again is
true as regards the old hatched flies. In fact, it
is a question in my mind whether every winged
insect in existence would not seek shelter to prevent its wings becoming sodden. But these are
not the grannoms on which the fish feed. The fish
sees rising through the water the nymph enveloped
in a thin skin, which skin splits on the surface
of the water, and the winged grannom flutters over
it until it reaches the bank in safety. Fish rising
at grannom are taking that fly in one of the
two above-mentioned states—either the nymph, or
the winged insect struggling on the water to get
safely to shore. The symptoms are unmistakable,
whether it be the nymph or the winged fly, as the
fish cannot poise themselves in the same way as
they do when taking duns and quietly suck in the

insect floating down to it. They keep darting backwards and forwards after the active nymph or the
fluttering imago ; in fact, altogether the appearance
is very like that of trout *bulging*. After the hatch
of winged grannom has once commenced (and the
first commencement is certainly retarded by unseason-
able weather) all this fair weather theory is blown
to the winds. Frequently on cold, wet, blustery
days the fly is well up, the fish are taking it well,
and especially if the surface of the water is rippled
by a moderate breeze the angler has a fair chance
of getting near his fish without being seen.

I venture to differ entirely from the common
theory of anglers that the grannom should be used
only in fine weather. The grannom is certainly a
capital fly to fatten the fish, but it is as certainly only
plentiful on a few streams, and is altogether a most
disappointing one to the anglers. On the days of
its biggest hatch, when a quiet part of the river is
simply one seething mass of struggling flies just
hatched, and empty shucks, and the fish are boiling
in all directions, the angler really does not know
which fish to try. It is almost impossible in such
a commotion for him to tell one from the other ;
in his hurry he generally selects the small fry,
and if by chance he should hook a big fish, the
general result is a smash, as, owing to the excitement of seeing so many trout rising and the disappointment of hooking small fellows one after the
other, at length he loses his coolness, and the

natural result is a little too much power in the strike.

Worse than all, perhaps, after a few minutes the fish are gorged and the rise for the day is at an end. Whenever, during the hatch of grannom, the trout are evidently not taking it, try one of the greener-bodied medium olives.

The commencement of May may be said to be the end of the grannom, sometimes even the best of it, and especially in cold seasons. We then come to a time of the year when the natural dun is paler in colour, and perhaps a trifle smaller, and such patterns as the hare's ear quill, the pale olive quill, the goose dun, and so on may be tried with advantage. On rough bright days the gold-ribbed hare's ear is the best and most reliable. In fact this sentence may be written without exception on every month in the year, and if a Hampshire fisher had to select one fly, and one fly only, on which to pin his faith he could not do better than take this.

Iron blues when hatching are specially successful at this period during the day; and for the evening, although there is not much evening rise as early as this, yet sometimes, when calm, the various forms of red spinner, red quills, detached badger, jenny spinners, and even occasionally the silver sedge may be tried with advantage.

The olive spinners are often out, but as far as my experience goes the fish do not take the natural well, and the imitation, as may be expected, is taken still worse. For patterns to resemble it, the olive badger is the most like nature, but perhaps a medium olive quill is quite as likely, if not more likely, to kill.

At the latter end of May the season of *curses* commences. Perhaps this word may be taken in both senses, as these horrible little midges seem the most provoking form of insect ever bred in the water. For patterns, the black gnat, both male and female, the pike scale, and the pattern given in "Floating Flies and how to Dress them" as the "Fisherman's Curse, A.," with body of cock golden pheasant tail, are the best imitations. As stated in a previous chapter, when fish are apparently taking minute flies, and the angler cannot discover the right pattern or see the insect itself, the orange bumble or furnace is always worth a trial. On some rivers smutting fish freely take a pink Wickham, tied quite small on a oo hook, and in connection with this point rather a curious circumstance should be noted. It is not only on some rivers that smutting fish take a pink Wickham, and on other rivers that they refuse it, but on some parts of the same stream. And, as an example, Houghton is a piece of water on which trout will very seldom take the Wickham; but on a small tributary of the same stream which I formerly rented I almost always found it successful. This, however, was not due to the fish being less shy, as I think I can honestly say that in no stream, or no part of any stream, even including Houghton

itself, had I found the fish so shy and so difficult as
on this particular piece of water. Sometimes where
they will not take the pink Wickham, a small red
quill or a small silver sedge may be successful,
although, as previously explained in a chapter on
the subject, it is a great mystery why, and for what,
these particular patterns are taken by fish which are
palpably, as shown by actual experiments in the
shape of autopsy, taking nothing but these little
black midges. I have seen sedges out quite early
in May, and have not only seen them, but have
killed with them. As an example, I note from my
diary that on the 19th May 1882, on a cold evening,
with a northerly wind, when I only arrived by train
at a few minutes before seven o'clock, and started
at once fishing, I killed with a silver sedge on a
o hook a trout 2 lbs. 4 ozs. at the very first cast,
and subsequently lost and rose several others. In
the last days of May sometimes the first appearance
of the green drake is noticed, with the accompanying
alder, button, sedge, &c.; but these flies belong to
June, and I will treat of them in detail under the
section of Summer.

SUMMER.

With the commencement of June in ordinary
seasons the first appearance of the May-fly may
be expected. Probably more inaccuracies and more
misleading matter have been given forth to the

public about this fly than on all other angling subjects. The May-fly fortnight used to be said, especially
by the older school of authors, to be a sort of carnival
—in fact, some have canonised it by the name of
St. May-fly; and to read their glowing sketches
one would fancy that it was only necessary to cast
the fly in any slipshod fashion anywhere, to find as
a result that all the big fish in the river were com-
peting in a race to get at it; and anglers, especially
of the younger school, reading these exaggerated accounts, are in the habit of going down to the river
buoying themselves up with hopes of great sport and
easy fishing. Some even say that it is unsportsman-
like, and describe it as a sort of poaching, as bad as
the minnow, worse than the worm, and only on a
par with the net. How soon they would be unde-
ceived if they only tried one season on the Test!
They would find that, really and truly speaking, it is
far more difficult than any ordinary fishing, not only
because of the mere labour of drying the fly and the
increased difficulty of casting so big an object against
the wind; not only because of the long hours of
daylight during which they stop out of doors and try
to keep on fishing; not only because of the heat of
the weather, but in addition to all this, because of
the fact that, as they well know, the big fish are
all on the move; of course every one's desire is to
catch the big ones, and these wary old customers
will not stand the smallest mistake.

On the other hand, experienced dry-fly fishermen

PLATE XV.

MAYFLY

Ephemera danica.

1
Eggs × 46.

2
Larva just hatched × 23.

3
Larva.

4
Nymph Female.

5
Nymph Male.

Kemp del.

Leighton Brothers, *Lith*.

among southern anglers have, for many seasons past, raised a general wail of discontent at the bad sport they have obtained during the short fortnight of the May-fly. Complaints on this score have been even more rife this year (1888) than previously, and hence, perhaps, a calm and judicial consideration of the various circumstances producing or tending to produce this undesirable result is not out of place here. It is said that trout do not take the natural fly as freely as was their wont in former days. I believe that this is not the case, and that the almost universal disappointment is due to a variety of causes, some natural and others preventable, brought about partly by want of experience and partly by the ever-increasing shyness of the fish, greatly increased by excessive or injudicious casting over them at all times and seasons.

The life-history of the May-fly has been exhaustively treated by many entomologists, notably by Pictet, and in later years by the Rev. A. E. Eaton, and a short *résumé*, as far as I have been able to verify the various statements from personal observation, may be acceptable to the reader. The eggs, an illustration of which, magnified forty-six diameters, is shown in Plate XV. 1, when first laid in the water sink to the bottom and adhere to the soil or stones forming the bed of the river, where they remain until hatched into a small grub or larva. How long this process of hatching takes is, more or less, a matter of conjecture. I can to a certain extent elucidate the question from positive experiments, as I secured a number of eggs from about 120 impregnated females, and an enthusiastic angling friend tried to hatch them in captivity in a small aquarium. These eggs were taken on the 9th of June 1887. They numbered, as nearly as could be calculated, about 800,000. This number may, at the first glance, appear to the reader to be an exaggeration, but the result of dissecting out and counting under the microscope the eggs from six females (three large and three small) gave respectively the following numbers: 6693, 6048, 7134, 5682, 5748, 7728; and these figures tally sufficiently closely to an average of 6500 eggs per fly, to show that this calculation is very nearly accurate. They were safely delivered into the hands of my friend (Mr. Hawksley), and carefully deposited by him in certain vessels for the purpose of hatching. On the 15th August, or about five weeks later, I received a most exciting telegram, " Cannot leave home; May-flies hatching." On the next day came a letter with full details stating that thousands had hatched, that the new-born larvæ were busy cleaning themselves and commencing to feed, that a certain number had been sacrificed in the cause of science, and were temporarily preserved in spirit for me. Thanks to this forethought I am able to give the accompanying illustration of the larva (magnified twenty-three diameters, on Plate XV. 2), when certainly less than one week old. Both Mr. Hawksley's and my own excitement about this time were very great. We were building hopes of at last (for we had previously hatched larva, but failed to rear them) working out in full detail the life-history of one of the Ephemeridæ. To provide as far as possible a fair imitation of their natural surroundings, I had brought up from Hampshire a quantity of mud taken from the bed of the river, and a number of various sorts of weeds growing there. These were carefully distributed in the various vessels.

The larvæ commenced to dig burrows into the sandy mud with their powerful forelegs, which are armed with formidable claws for the purpose, and altogether we began to think that our experiment showed fair signs of being successful, especially as we knew that throughout the larval and nymph stages the May-fly takes up its habitation in the mud. After a few weeks a careful search in one of the vessels showed us not a single sign of a larva. This naturally gave rise to considerable anxiety, and we could not be satisfied with anything less than an exhaustive search, which, alas! proved that our very worst apprehensions were only too well founded.

Excepting the small number of larvæ preserved in spirit, we could only find one other specimen. Our want of success was probably due to a variety of causes, notably ignorance of the natural diet of the insect, and the impossibility of producing in the circumscribed area of a small aquarium in a London

greenhouse the same conditions, the same atmosphere, the same flow of fresh water, and possibly
the same pure water filtered through the chalk as
in its native river.

Be that as it may, we failed; and our only remedy
is to try again, with hopes of better results. Strange
to say, however, some months later a number of
eggs were found which had not hatched, and yet,
under the microscope, gave every indication of being
alive. These eggs were treated in the same careful
manner, but having shown no change whatever up
to June 1888, a period of twelve months from the
date of being laid, we concluded that, from some
unexplained cause, they were unfertile eggs, and
hence we reluctantly decided to destroy them. Experiments, however, are still being conducted on
the subject, and will, I trust, eventually prove successful, elucidating the question as to the period
which elapses between the laying of the egg and the
appearance of the sub-imago or winged fly.

As the larva grows it sheds its outside skin many
times, and at some period of its growth it commences to assume the nymph state. Plate XV. 3 is
a coloured illustration of the larva life-size, and Nos.
4 and 5 on the same plate are the female and male
nymph respectively. On Plate XVI. the larva and
both sexes of nymph are shown magnified three
diameters. The only apparent difference between
the larva and the nymph is the appearance in
the latter of two small oval-shaped excrescences of

PLATE XVI.

MAYFLY

(*Ephmera danica*)

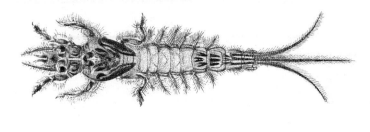
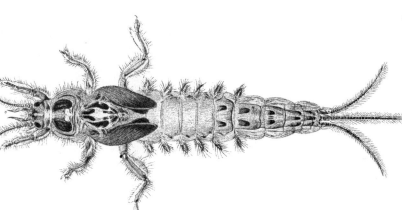

Larva × 3.

Nymph Female × 3.

Nymph Male × 3.

E.Kemp, del.

Leighton Brothers. *Lith*.

a dark colour, springing from the back of the thorax. These are, in fact, cases in which the wings of the sub-imago are curiously folded up, somewhat in the same way as an umbrella is folded for the purpose of carrying when not in use. There is some doubt in my mind as to the correctness, from a scientific point of view, of the use of these two names, larva and nymph, as indicating, one the immature insect *without*, and the other the immature insect *with*, the small wing-covers ; but as their meaning is explained they are convenient terms, and hence my scientific friends will perhaps forgive me if I am guilty of a misnomer.

As the weather becomes colder the larva digs its way more deeply into the soil. In the depths of winter it is said to be immersed as much as a yard or more in the soft mud, and in more genial weather it is found usually at a depth of about eighteen inches. As an illustration of this I may state that, in the month of March 1887, my friend Major Turle sent me from Newton Stacey, his water on the Test, specimens found at a depth of from a foot to eighteen inches below the surface of the mud, and a fortnight later, when a sudden change of weather had caused a very decided fall of temperature, could not get any more when dredging to the depth of nearly a yard. Entomologists are somewhat vague as to the length of time during which the insect remains in the larval and nymph dresses. This is certainly not less than two years, as in the second

M

week of June larvæ have been found by me without
any sign of the wing-covers, and not more than one-
half the length of the full-grown nymphæ, when at
the same time the winged fly was prevalent on the
water.

When the time to be spent in the larval state has
come to a close, however long it may be, the nymphæ
are found among the roots and the weeds in the
sandy mud at a depth of about an inch. This fact,
as noticed in the *Field* of 2d July 1887, was witnessed by me in person, and perhaps I may be
excused for quoting the paragraph *in extenso* :—

" MAY-FLY METAMORPHOSIS.—In my May-fly notes
of June 4th the following sentence occurs :—The
larvæ of *Ephemera danica*,[1] from the time of their
first emerging from the eggs to about a month or so
before undergoing the further metamorphosis to the
sub-imago, burrow deeply into the mud, and there
take up their habitations. My reason for accepting
the period of a month or so before assuming the sub-
imago state was because I could get no reliable information on this point, and had not been able to
satisfy myself as to the habits of the larvæ or nymphæ
when approaching the transformation to a winged
insect. Fortunately, however, I met on one of the
waters fished last week a remarkably intelligent

---

[1] In the original this May-fly was named *Ephemera vulgata*, but I
prefer to follow the nomenclature of the Rev. A. E. Eaton, the best
modern authority on this family, who gives as its scientific name
E. danica. The May-fly of warmer rivers is usually *E. vulgata* (Eaton)
or, more rarely, *E. lineata*.

keeper, who assured me that the larvæ were then about an inch below the surface of the mud around the roots of the weeds. At my request he scooped out several bunches of weed with roots and mud attached, and after leaving them a few moments on the bank the head and shoulders of the nymphæ emerged from the soil, and I preserved several specimens for future observations under the microscope. The wing-cases were fully developed, and one nympha actually underwent the metamorphosis under my eyes, splitting open the larval envelope between the shoulders, then lifting out its head and legs, then curving its body upwards and drawing it out, together with the setæ ; and lastly, unfolding the wings as they emerged from the wing-cases, it fluttered away, to fall a victim to the open jaws of a hungry swallow. This information is of great value to owners of fisheries who are bothered by the various opinions expressed on the subject of weed-cutting just before the May-fly season. They can now safely cut away all superfluous weeds, in full confidence of not hindering the hatch of drakes and spoiling their sport in the early days of June." [1]

This description of the process of metamorphosis to the sub-imago is, I believe, accurate, and I would only add that the powerful digging claws, the whole of the mouth appendages, and the branchiæ or gill

[1] I may here acknowledge, with many thanks, the courtesy of the proprietors of the *Field* in according me permission to use this and other matter which has appeared in that invaluable sportsman's Bible.

apparatus used for separating air from the water for breathing purposes, are shed with the exuviæ of the nymphæ; and the hairs with which the antennæ, legs, setæ, and parts of the body itself are fringed in the larval state are absent from the sub-imago.

In a state of nature, as soon as the wings of the sub-imago or green drake are thoroughly dried, it flies to the shore. During the process of drying its wings it is frequently seen floating on the surface of the stream, using the nymph envelope as a supporting raft. When ashore the sub-imago rests on the under side of leaves or on blades of grass, selecting invariably the shady side; in fact, at this period of its existence it seems especially to shun the burning rays of the sun. Nos. 1 and 2 of the accompanying Plate XVII. are correct representations of female and male at this stage drawn under the microscope, and reduced to the natural size, and Plate XVIII., 1 and 2, are the female and male sub-imago magnified three diameters. After about twenty-four to thirty-six hours, the time being, I believe, entirely dependent on temperature, the green drake casts the entire outer skin of its head, wings, thorax, and abdomen, as well as the thin coverings of the antennæ, legs, and setæ, the forelegs and setæ increasing very much in length, and the increase being relatively far greater in the males than in the females. The wings of the sub-imago are covered with small thorn-shaped spines all over the surface, and hairs along the edges, but the

PLATE XVII.

MAYFLY

Ephemera danica.

1
Subimago Female.

2
Subimago Male.

3
Imago Female.

4
Imago Male.

wings of the imago or perfect insect are comparatively smooth and free from these excrescences,
which are shed with the sub-imago envelope. The
imago, male and female, is shown on Plate XVII.,
3 and 4, the natural size, and Plates XIX. and XX.
show the female and male imago respectively magnified three diameters. It is curious to note that the
clouds of imago rising and falling in the air are exclu-
sively collections of males. As the sun gets low in
the horizon and the air begins to cool the males come
out in clouds, congregating together ; and, dancing up
and down, lie in wait for and catch each female as she
flies out into the open in the imago state. Sexual
intercourse takes place in the air, and very shortly
after it the female drops her eggs on the water, and
the act of reproduction being complete, both sexes
fall almost lifeless on the surface of the stream,
with their wings extended and lying flat ; and
their bodies, mere empty shells, are at this stage,
by a strange misnomer, called by anglers the *spent
gnat*.

A retrospect of the life-history of the May-fly will
show that the larvæ and nymphæ while burrowing in
the mud cannot to any large extent serve as food for
the fish. Hence the first stage at which it is possible
for the trout to feed on them freely is that of the
nymph at the moment it is rising to the surface of
the water as a preliminary to the change into the
winged insect. Thus, from an angler's point of view,
the consideration of the subject divides itself natu-

rally into the three states of nymph, sub-imago, and imago.

In the first of these states what is usually, but erroneously, called the hatch of the May-fly has just commenced. The first of the nymphæ are swimming upwards in all directions, and the trout, who are probably not endowed by nature with the faculty of memory from past years, are scared at the sight of this strange and large creature. After a time curiosity probably impels them to try it from a gastronomic point of view, and the first mouthful proving tasty is soon succeeded by others, until at length all over the stream the fish are feeding ravenously on the succulent and highly nutritious nymphs. The evidences of this are unmistakable —a noisy splashing *floop* continually recurring, with frequent changes of position as the hungry trout chase the active nymphs; but there is very seldom an actual breaking of the surface except when the nymph reaches the top of the water and splits the shuck at the very moment the fish is in the act of taking it, when he quickly secures either the winged insect or the empty envelope. It is a strange circumstance, too, that the fish often take the empty shuck in preference to the nymph itself.

The above is what happens in a river neglected by man. In civilised parts the first appearance of the fly is rapidly communicated by letter or telegram from the zealous keeper, and spread far and wide by the sporting press. Everywhere the cry, "The fly is up," is raised; every angler renting water or having the privilege of fishing on club or private ground is off by the next train, anxious to be first on the spot. The fish, long before they have settled down to feed on the fly—in fact often before they are thoroughly sure of the flavour of the nymph—are cast over time after time, pricked whenever a mistake is made, and a certain proportion killed. They are scared by the sudden influx of people on the banks of the streams comparatively deserted at other times, until at length the natural result is to render them preternaturally shy and drive them off surface food for very fear of their lives.

In private waters the remedy is simple, and it is in the owner's hands. He should himself abstain from fishing until the trout have become accustomed to the winged fly, and the abstinence he practised himself could not be a great hardship to his friends. In subscription or club waters, however, this is impossible, for although, as a class, anglers are unselfish and considerate towards their *confrères*, there would, I fear, in each case be some one or more greedy members who would strive to get a start and distance their more considerate fellow-members. If, therefore, obliged in self-defence to try the fish in this stage, there are a few simple rules which should materially increase the bag of the fisherman.

For the fish when feeding on the nymphæ a

new pattern, and a most efficacious one, has been
recently evolved by Mr. Marryat. It is dressed
without wings, with Egyptian goose hackle, body
of the palest buff, maize-coloured floss silk, ribbed
with a strand of peacock's herl, which is of pale
cinnamon colour at the root. The pale portion
of the herl is worked at the shoulders so as to show
about three turns of the dark metallic bronze at the
tail end of the body, which very fairly represents the
darker marking on this portion of the natural fly.
The tail is of brown mallard, or gallina, dyed to this
colour. It is, however, a very difficult fly to dress,
owing to the stubborn nature of the stem of the
Egyptian goose hackle. If this pattern is not available, an ordinary straw-bodied small May-fly, with
wings of the tint known as Hammond's champion,
is a very good substitute. In any case the fly
should not be too dry, although, at the same time,
it should not actually sink below the surface, and
when using the winged pattern it is above all essential to fish it with the wings flat upon the water
and not cocked. Any experienced fisherman can,
after a few trials, manage to achieve this, and I
would refer the novice to a previous chapter, which
will indicate the best method of delivering the fly
so that it shall not be cocked. This is done by
either casting over hand, which perhaps is not desirable, or putting a little superfluous force into the
throw. Two or three accurate casts delicately
made, and the fly placed well above the fish, are

PLATE XVIII.

MAYFLY.

(*Ephemera danica.*)

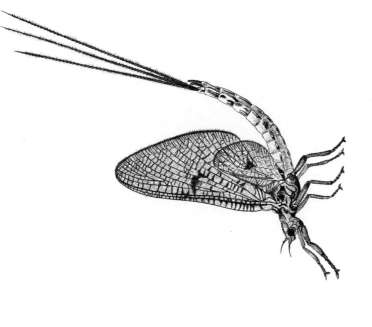

Subimago Male × 3.

Subimago Female × 3.

quite sufficient. To go on flogging after this is simply to educate the trout, and ruin your own sport, as well as that of others. If after two or three casts the fly is not taken, wait, rest your fish, let him get the flavour again of a few naturals, then give him the artificial two or three times. If still unable to tempt him, crawl back from the bank so as not to show yourself and scare him, and go and find another fish, returning to your old friend in half an hour's time. If, however, the river has been left alone until the fish are really well on the sub-imago or green drake, then great sport may be expected for some days during the prevalence of the fly. It is well to note the hour at which the rise takes place, and in settled weather it will be found as a general rule that this hour becomes later from day to day. Observation of this point will save unnecessary fatigue.

When trout are taking the green drake there can be no possible doubt about it. The fly is floating down continually, fish after fish take up their positions and suck in quietly without splash or disturbance one after another, and this is the time to make a bag. It must be remembered, however, that a very small mistake is enough to set a rising fish down, so that the well-known and oft-repeated maxim of *accuracy and delicacy combined in the first cast* is most essential, and an absolutely dry fly cocked a positive necessity to ensure success.

As to patterns, " their name is legion." The

majority of them are good. Perhaps the best of
all is the straw-bodied champion; and the undyed
Rouen drake-wing, with straw body, or Canadian
summer duck wings may be tried for a change.
Professionals as a rule, however, dress their May-flies
on hooks many sizes too large and out of all proportion to the natural insect. Compare a champion on
a No. 2 hook with a live fly, and it will be seen that
it is quite as large as—in fact, a trifle larger than—
the male green drake; and one on a No. 3-long is
exaggerated as to size when compared with a very
large female. It is true that fish will rise at these
colossal specimens of the fly-dresser's art; but it is
equally true that they rise shyly and without confidence, *floop* at it, and do not take it, or are only
pricked, and are spoiled for hours at least, or sometimes even for the whole season. Too great stress
cannot be laid on the necessity of modern anglers
purchasing only May-flies dressed on small hooks,
and thus curing professionals once for all of their
silly mania for turning out such disproportioned
imitations.

Weather is probably credited with having far too
much effect upon this as well as all other classes of
fly fishing. In rain it certainly is difficult to dry the
fly, but, on the other hand, the fish take better in
cloud or gloom than in sunshine. To cast so large
a fly with more than, say, a yard and a half of gut
against a strong down-stream wind is impossible;
but, as a consolation, an up-stream wind lifts the

natural fly off the water almost the moment it is clear of the shuck, while with a down-stream wind it sails along steadily, and is more easily secured by the fish; also, as remarked in a previous chapter, it is more easy to cock the fly when casting against the wind. Again, the advice is repeated not to keep on hammering away at a rising trout. Keep out of sight, crouching well down on approaching the bank, and while fishing or retiring. Use the under-hand cast invariably, and although fine gut is desirable, it is not so absolutely essential as when using duns or other small flies. One other hint. Sometimes the fish are not taking the natural May-fly well and yet rise occasionally, and under these conditions it is better to try first with Flight's fancy, or some other small fly. Very few casts will tell whether these are likely to be successful, and if not, do not hesitate for a moment; put up either an alder or a Welshman's button, both of which are almost invariably found at the same time as the May-fly, especially for half an hour just before the rise of the green drake.

If neither of these is successful, a sedge will often prove of service in converting an unfavourable into a favourable day's sport. Of the efficacy of the Welshman's button I had curious evidence some years ago when fishing on a very good piece of private water. My friend who was with me on that occasion, and who is quite in the first school of Hampshire May-fly fishers, had been trying a fish rising on the edge of a run for some time, fishing scientifically, and to my notion very well. When I arrived on the spot he was grumbling at his bad luck in not being able to get a rise, and exclaiming that probably our host had either pricked or hammered the fish on the previous day. A few moments before I had killed a fish with a Welshman's button, and as he had previously refused a *champion*, I suggested to my friend a change to the button. He is generally an advocate for sticking to the fly on the water, and not seeing any of these particular insects, somewhat scornfully said, " You had better try him yourself." My first cast was certainly not a good one—that is to say, it was not an accurate one, as the fly was coming down on the extreme right-hand side of the run, while the fish was rising on the extreme left ; yet he came right across the run, seized the fly, and was killed in a few minutes—a good trout of about $2\frac{1}{2}$ lbs.

During the hatch of the May-fly, especially the earlier portion of it, there will often be seen of an evening a small number of large red sedges. I say a small number advisedly, as, with the utmost diligence when hunting for it, I have only succeeded in getting in the last two years some twelve or fourteen specimens. A pattern of sedge which I have called the *Kimbridge* as a modification of a pattern previously dressed and called by that name, seems to me the best imitation of that large sedge. I dress it on a 3-long hook, with wings of woodcock, body of

PLATE XIX.

MAYFLY

Ephemera danica.

Imago Female × 3.

E.Kemp del.   Leighton Brothers, *Lith*.

pale condor—not absolutely white—and rib it right
down with two pale ginger hackles. This pattern
has proved so successful in killing large fish during
the evening rise, and sometimes too in the middle of
the day, when the May-fly itself has not seemed to
tempt the trout, that I think it worthy the attention
of my brother anglers.

When feeding on the spent gnat or imago in the
final stage of its existence a trout usually takes
up its position close to the surface, and swimming
leisurely along with his nose almost out of the
water, quietly sucks in every fly drifting down.
The flies scarcely move, and are apparently lifeless,
so that the disturbance even of the largest fish is
unimportant, and the mark made by the rise of a
four-pounder a mere bubble, like the rise of a minnow. It is usually late in the day or evening, perhaps nearly dusk; the wind has died away; everything is calm and placid. In the deep, slow, or even
almost stagnant water, the fish, and frequently the
very largest ones, are only submerged a few inches
under the surface, and swim slowly along taking
every spent gnat they see. They cruise about a
good deal when feeding in this way, and it is
desirable to watch the wave of the trout, and thus
ascertaining the direction in which he is moving,
cast about a foot above him. Under these conditions
it is not surprising that the smallest splash, the least
curve in the gut, the shadow of the moving rod, or
the slightest suspicion of anything abnormal, is suffi-

cient to show a danger-signal which promptly moves the trout already gorged with food to seek safety in a quick retreat.

As to the imitation, no spent gnat pattern can be considered in the same category as that invented by friend Marryat as the result of life-long study. It is, as is well known to Hampshire anglers, dressed with wings lying horizontally at right angles to the hook-shank, and formed with four transparent blue Andalusian grizzled cock hackle points, body of white floss silk ribbed with a cinnamon-ended strand of peacock, whisks of brown mallard or gallina dyed a dark brown nearly black, a grey partridge hackle at the shoulder, and a badger cock hackle carried down the body from the shoulder to the tail end. For choice it should be dressed on nothing larger than 3-long hook, and for very shy fish even smaller.

When to cast is an important point. The natural fly usually floats down in a string of twenty or more close together. A fish will take every one of such a series, and then go down to swallow the mass. The artificial should, therefore, be thrown at the moment the string of natural flies is approaching, so that it will lead the file. If it is not taken the first cast, wait and let your fish take another lot of the natural before trying again. Sometimes, if this is unsuccessful, a cast a foot to the right or left of the drift of natural flies will tempt him ; but if this, in turn, is of no avail, pass on and try another fish. Above all, do not keep on casting over the same fish. It is utterly useless, and worse still as only tending to render a shy fish still more suspicious. The largest fish are killed with a spent gnat when they do take it; and as an example, some few years ago one of 8 lbs. was secured with it, and the following season one of 7 lbs. in very nearly the same spot. And yet altogether it is the most disappointing style of fishing. Perhaps, as a consolation, we may think it just as well that the big fish only take it freely at rare intervals; otherwise, with the present plethora of sportsmen, the race would in many rivers soon be extinct. Occasionally the trout take the spent gnat well in the morning, especially after a very great show of green drake over night; so after the first few days with the fly it is always worth while to try it when unable to get a rise with the May-fly itself.

One more hint. If you happen to be fishing on a stream a week or so after the May-fly is over, and find a fish rising at duns or other small insects, and cannot succeed in tempting him, do not hesitate to give him one cast with the May-fly or spent gnat. The memory of the taste seems to linger in their minds for some short time.

On rivers where no May-fly hatches, or where they are not sufficiently plentiful to make the fish feed on them, June is generally a good month. Moderately early in the morning, say seven o'clock perhaps, the claret spinner or detached badger will often

take. Not so often, but yet occasionally, the jenny
spinner. This circumstance seems to me somewhat
strange, as one is the female imago and the other
the male imago of one and the same fly, the iron
blue. During the day-time, if there is any small
fly rise, Flight's fancy, medium or pale olives, iron
blues, sometimes orange bumbles, and furnaces will
take. The alder is a fly which is always worth
trying, as on most rivers there is more or less of
it about from the middle of May to the middle of
June. In the evenings red spinners, detached bad-
gers, red quills, badger quills, and after dark various
patterns of sedges, not forgetting Hammond's adopted,
the artful dodger, or our old friend the Kimbridge,
mentioned when speaking of the May-fly, or imitation
of the large red sedge, which is only seen at this
time of the year.

Of July there is not much to be said. Altogether
it is perhaps the worst month in the year for killing
trout in the day-time. In rivers where the May-fly
is plentiful they have scarcely recovered from it.
They are fat and lazy and generally shy, and in all
rivers, whether those where there is or is not much
May-fly, duns are very scarce. If there is any rise
at all the flies are small, and must be dressed on
oo or ooo hooks ; the finest of drawn gut must be
used ; and at a time when the weeds are thick and
strong, when the fish are in the pink of condition
and have a strong tendency to go to weed and to
smash the angler when there, it is not easy to hold

PLATE XX.

MAYFLY
Ephemera danica.

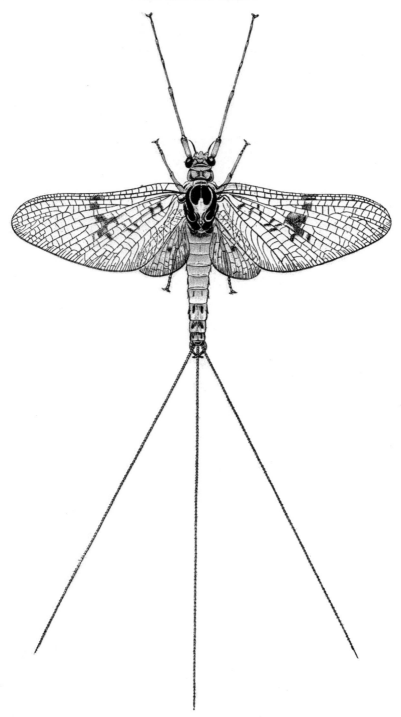

Kemp, del.

Imago Male × 3.

Leighton Brothers, *Lith.*

them, and the general disappointment experienced by fishermen is not altogether surprising.

Sometimes grayling take well in July, but they should not, to my notion, be killed earlier than the middle, or at very earliest the commencement, of the month. The fact that they do feed well in July is a strong argument in favour of having them in streams with the trout, providing the stock of food is plentiful. Of course, if there is not a sufficiency of insect life to form food for both trout and grayling, and the river will only support a certain head of fish the effect is not satisfactory, as the grayling, who certainly increase far more rapidly than trout, seem to take an unfair share of the food and crowd out the *salmo fario*. The grayling take red tag, macaw tag, orange tag, orange bumble, furnace, curse, black gnat, Wickham, small silver sedge, and even Sanctuary tied on a large No. 2 hook. These patterns for day-time only. In the early evenings both trout and grayling sometimes rise well, taking all sorts of red spinners, blue-winged olive when it is out, and, of course, its imago, the sherry spinner, which is best imitated by a somewhat pale-bodied red spinner or detached badger. When it gets almost dark the grayling, as a rule, do not take, and rising fish may be generally considered to be trout. They should first be tried with silver sedge on a o hook. If this is unsuccessful a hare's ear sedge of the same size; then as it gets darker either the silver or hare's

N

ear sedge on a No. 2 hook; and when quite dark,
some of the larger sedges, such as Hammond's
adopted, artful dodger, or the dark sedge dressed
on hooks about No. 4.

AUTUMN.

To include the month of August under Autumn
is perhaps not strictly correct, yet I do so advisedly,
because the particular style of feeding on the part
of the trout begins in that month to partake of the
character which I would describe as specially ap-
pertaining to this season. They certainly seem in
better appetite and far less shy than they were in
July in the day-time. Of course the same small
flies dressed on oo and ooo hooks on finest gut,
with the addition of the Indian yellow, little Marryat,
and cinnamon quill are the prevalent patterns of
duns. Sometimes, if the weather be very sultry and
very calm, I have found the black and red ants
useful flies during the heat of the day, especially
the red. As to evening fishing, it is distinctly good,
and the night fishing, if I can call the period just
after dusk so, even better.

Success or non-success in fishing after dusk depends
entirely on the presence of sedge flies, and the later
we are in the season the more prevalent are the natural insects; in fact, I think there are more to be seen
in October than any month in the year. Very fine
gut is not necessary; in fact, one may use strong

undrawn, there being no advantage in handicapping yourself at a time when the gut is probably far less visible to the fish than during daylight. It is also well to note that no place in which a fish is feeding need be passed over on account of the natural difficulties of landing him when hooked, as even in parts almost entirely overgrown with weed, with mere patches between, trout may be frequently killed, as they very seldom go to weed after dark. Probably this is accounted for by the fact of the fisherman being invisible until they are almost tired out and practically in the net; and weeding is, I believe, in many cases, the result of a scare on the part of the trout from seeing the fisherman.

In September the trout, especially the large ones, are in real good fettle, and often take well from morning to night. Candidly, I think it is very doubtful whether it is wise policy to kill them on comparatively early rivers like the Test; and after, say, the 15th, I feel certain that proprietors of fisheries would be doing good by ending their season. This assertion is based on a somewhat careful study of the subject. Some years back I suspected, and since then continual examination from season to season has convinced me, that by far the majority of the fish killed in the latter half of September are females getting heavy with roe. The result of killing any great number of these must obviously be to unduly decrease the stock of fish likely to spawn at the end of the year.

The flies for trout in September are exactly as in August. The grayling run a good average, fight well, being in good condition, and take from sunrise to sunset. They are always somewhat difficult to please, and require great variety of fly. It is surprising how a little perseverance and continual changing of pattern will enable one angler to make a good day among them, while his brother anglers on the same stream who are sticklers for using only a good imitation of the natural fly on the water get little or no sport. Of the various duns, the small red, blue, olive, and cinnamon quills, little Marryat, Indian yellow, Wickham, and small silver sedge are about the best. The black gnats, curses, various patterns of red and orange tags, and bumbles are all good for a change. Occasionally, but very seldom, grayling take the sedge well just at dusk. On very hot days, at times, they will take it comparatively early in the afternoon.

With the end of September at the latest trout fishing should close on every southern stream; in fact, Francis Francis's " Anathema Maranatha" on those who will kill grayling in June is not half scathing enough for those who will kill trout in October. No matter in how perfect a condition they may seem to be, yet within an hour of their being dead they are flabby, dark-coloured, and loathsome objects. For the table they are utterly useless; and although some so-called sportsmen salve their consciences by declaring the trout they kill in Octo-

ber are barren ones, yet I confess I should not care
to trust gentlemen who profess to be so wise on this
point.   Certainly one provoking feature about it
is, that the trout rise well, and not only rise well,
but take well; and in addition to all this, when one
lands a trout in October it frequently is a very large
one for the stream.   Yet all who wish their stock of
fish to have a fair chance of multiplying and being
fruitful should make a rigid rule of returning them
in this month.   Of course, fish rising close under
the banks should be avoided, as they are generally
trout.

It may be a consolation, however, that grayling
are not only in the best condition, and hence fight
better, in October than in any other month in the
year, but all of them, from the largest to the smallest,
are feeding freely.   Thus the best sport may be anticipated by the fisherman who determines to treat grayling fishing as a serious branch of the subject, who
uses small flies and fine gut, who fishes dry over rising
fish, and who avoids the dreadful theory perpetrated
by some of our northern friends that grayling fishing
consists in throwing at haphazard two sunk flies
down-stream anywhere.   All that may be truly called
grayling patterns are good ones in this month.   The
adjutant blue, perhaps, is the best, and very nearly
allied to it are the autumn dun and blue quill.   Tags,
bumbles, Wickhams, and even blacks are sometimes successful.   The little Marryat, cinnamon
quill, and Indian yellow are all reliable standards in

Hampshire; and on very rare occasions the willow
fly, but not often. This elegant member of the
Perlidæ family is, however, said to be a favourite
with grayling elsewhere, especially in Yorkshire,
Derbyshire, and other parts of the Midlands. It
is, however, not an easy pattern to imitate; and to
appreciate the difficulty, it is only necessary for the
angler to note the difference in appearance between
two specimens, one flying through the air with its
four wings extended and fluttering, and the other
crawling up a post or over a bridge, and looking like
a fragment of annealed iron wire, whence probably
the north country name for it of *needle brown* is
derived. Late in the afternoon red quills, red
spinners, and silver sedges are possible chances
for sport.

In the two concluding months of the year,
November and December, the larger grayling are
not generally rising, and those which rise often
take duns, gold-ribbed hare's ear, or blue quill for
choice. Sometimes there is an off chance with
Indian yellow, little Marryat, Wickham, adjutant, or
autumn duns; and when the fish are rising and
no flies can be seen on the water, it is perhaps well
to try tags, bumbles, and such fancy flies, but they
are certainly not uniformly as successful as duns
at this season of the year. Cold weather does not
always prevent the grayling from rising well. I had
heard this assertion many years ago, and, candidly,
misjudged the sportsman who made it; but ex-

perience has since taught me that he was not far wrong. And perhaps my own doings of two days, the 28th and 29th November 1884, may be of interest as tending to show what sport one may have on such days. I killed on the 28th, a comparatively mild day, nine grayling weighing 9 lbs. 13 ozs. At sunset it became very cold and cloudy. After a time snow began to fall, and continued throughout the night. In the morning the ground was covered to a depth of nearly a foot. It was bitterly cold, and snowing off and on until midday. It then cleared up, but was still very cold, although the sun broke through occasionally. About one o'clock a few large olives were hatching; but it was still freezing; indeed, I think it froze all day long. About half-past one the fish began rising, and within twenty minutes, fishing with a gold-ribbed hare's ear, I killed six grayling, weighing together 8 lbs. 7 ozs., the best and last one of 2¾ lbs., and lost five or six more; and such sport, I think, as this would be sufficient to tempt any angler, even in a severe frost.

I am told that grayling rise well on mild days up to Christmas, although I have not fished as late as that. After that date the river should be rested until the opening of the trout season. The trout as soon as they have done spawning are hungry, and whenever there is anything like a rise of fly they naturally feed and get pricked; some perhaps are hooked and returned, and so made even more shy than usual. In fact, I doubt whether after the end of November it is really worth trying at all excepting on particularly favourable days. It is also well to give the keepers plenty of time to attend to various details on the water, such as removing heavy patches of weed, repairing bridges, renovating planks, and generally making improvements in the state of the fishery, and the time between Christmas and the opening of the trout season is, to my mind, by no means too long for that purpose.

CHAPTER IX.

EVENING FISHING.

As the days lengthen at the end of the spring the water usually gets lower and brighter, and the trout from day to day become more and more gut shy, and when they do take flies they are smaller and smaller, until at last it becomes almost impossible to do any good at all in the day-time, except, of course, on streams or parts of streams where the fly fisherman is a *rara avis*, or possibly on an occasional cloudy, rainy, or windy day. The quantity of Ephemeridæ hatching also becomes smaller and smaller, for they do not, as a rule, change from the nymph to the sub-imago state in great numbers in the heat of the sun. This, possibly, is to some extent due to instinct on their part, as the sub-imago appears unwilling to expose itself for any length of time to great heat.

Under these conditions the best chance of getting sport is probably during what is called the evening rise. Now this evening rise is divided into two sections, the evening rise proper, or the time during which the fish are feeding on Ephemeridæ in either the sub-imago or imago stage, and the sedge rise, or time during which the fish are as a rule affecting flies of the Phryganidæ family. The true evening rise, that of the small fly, usually commences about the time that the lower limb of the sun touches the horizon. It will begin somewhat earlier on parts of the river where there is a hill on the western side or a high bank, producing a sort of artificial acceleration of sunset; and this rise continues just a little later than it is possible for one to see the artificial fly when throwing towards the light. About this period there is a lull for a quarter of an hour or so, during which the fish apparently are not taking much surface food. After this they come on to the smaller Phryganidæ. After some quarter or half an hour of this the larger sedge class are beginning to hatch, and seem to be taken more freely by the fish than any other.

It is evident that the small fly rise, or, as it is usually styled at Winchester, "Tom Fool's light," from the supposed facility with which fish can be killed, cannot, under the most favourable circumstances, last much more than half an hour. Fish during this period are almost as particular as to the colour of the fly, its shape, its size, or of its being dry and cocked (though they do not seem to mind the gut so much), as during the day-time. It would appear, therefore, that a fish's power of discrimination of colours is not to a very great extent impaired by partial loss of light, possibly owing to the lens of a fish's eye being capable of adjustment to a wider range, and consequently able to work through a denser medium than that of animals living in the air. Now, seeing the short time that this rise lasts, it is evidently an essential point that the first selection of fly should not be far out. The red spinners of various sorts, by which I mean such flies as red quill, detached badger, brown badger, and so on, and some of the yellow-bodied and even white duns, are the most useful.

There is occasionally on hot evenings a little white fly, somewhat similar both in colour and shape to the jenny spinner, but smaller, and the wings distinctly more rounded in shape. It is certainly much smaller than the jenny spinner, and on the evenings when it hatches comes out in tremendous swarms. I mention this fly because so many have noticed it, and so few seem to have taken the trouble of ascertaining anything about it. As far as my personal experience goes, and as far as I have been able to check it by the experience of other anglers, I have not been successful in finding one authenticated instance of its being taken by the fish; yet, at the same time, I think it is very probable that they take it; and possibly the reason of my not having been able to find it in any autopsy is, either that it is very rapidly digested, or, far more probably, that fish feeding on it will take nothing else; and thus, being unable to dress an imitation of so minute an object, I have failed to tempt them when taking it. This fly is one of the genus *Cænis*, probably either *Cænis rivulorum* (Eaton) or *C. lactea* (Pictet). Many of the Hampshire fishermen have a singular delusion about this fly, being of opinion that it bites. Now, a greater absurdity than this cannot exist, because, like all the Ephemeridæ in the winged state, the mouth organs are so atrophied that it would be utterly impossible. The reason of this fancied unpleasant tendency of these flies is due to the fact that they remain for a very short time in the sub-imago state, and wanting to change their coats, settle on the nearest object, whether it be a man's hand or his face, and as they settle they instinctively dig their claws into the substance on which they have settled for the purpose of fixing the claws of the sub-imago exuvium, to enable them to wriggle out of it and emerge an imago.

Possibly the reason of flies of the red spinner species killing well during the early evening rise is due to the fact that the majority of Ephemeridæ on the water are in the imago stage. It is possible that the cooling of the air after a hot summer's day kills or weakens them, and it is well known that the hotter the day, as a rule, the better is the evening rise, provided there is no mist. There is another reason, and most likely the best one, for accounting for the great numbers of spinners on the water, in the fact that, having laid their eggs, and thus fulfilled their province of reproduction, their life is at an end, and they fall on the water with their wings flat.

This flat-winged state in which they appear on the water is to my mind one of the strongest arguments

in favour of dressing spinners hackle or buzz fashion.
They should have plenty of hackle, although hackle
flies float very much better than one would think,
but are a little more difficult to see. As for time of
year, June, July, August, and even September are
the best months for this style of fishing.

On some evenings the various smuts are very
strong on the water, and although, as a rule, they
are not used by anglers, I think it is very possible
that they might be with advantage ; and my reasons
for expressing this opinion may be best given by the
illustration of an incident which happened to me on
the 1st August 1887. I was fishing the lower part
of the Houghton Water, on what is called the mill
pond, and noticed a number of fish rising. My
friend was quite sure they were dace, that is, after he
had made a few casts and failed to obtain a rise from
any of them, and suggested going on. I said, " No ;
I should be sorry to be contradictory, but I do not
think those are dace." The natural rejoinder was,
" Well, try them yourself." I had a detached badger
on with which I had been killing very fairly for
the previous evening or two, and crept quietly up
into position to the lowest fish. The fish were
rising one below, the other in one run. About the
second cast I hooked a fish, and at the first rush I
suggested to my friend that the dace in these parts
were of somewhat colossal dimensions, and eventually
he netted for me a grayling over a pound and three-
quarters. The very next cast I hooked a second

grayling over 2 lbs., and got him out. My friend, encouraged by this, thought he would have a try at these dace, and killed a grayling just under one pound and three-quarters; and by this time I think that we had set down the remainder of those which had been rising. We, however, walked up a short distance, when I saw a fish rising close under the opposite bank. My friend somewhat dared me to try him, and although perhaps it was not good judgment, as it was a longish throw, I did throw, and was fortunate enough to put the fly right, after the second or third cast, and killed a trout just under one pound and a half. When at home I spent some time in making an autopsy of every one of these fish, and with the exception of a few larvæ and a beetle or two in the grayling, the whole undigested contents of their stomachs consisted of nothing but smuts of different sorts and sizes.

The blue-winged olive is a fly which, although frequently out of an evening, especially from about the last week in July, is not as a rule successful; this, for one reason, probably because we have not found a really good imitation of it. The colour, especially of the body, is very peculiar, and I confess that none that I have yet seen have been really dyed to that shade. This fly is known to modern entomologists as *Ephemerella ignita*. Its imago, which is usually known to anglers by the name of the sherry spinner, is only imitated moderately well by a very pale or faded detached badger.

The natural fly carries a bunch of eggs of a blue-green colour at the penultimate section of the abdomen, holding them in position by its three setæ, which are turned forwards under the body, and hence barely visible. When flying in the air carrying these eggs they look very like ants, and until we caught them we always fancied they were ants. They are generally heading up-stream, and when they are seen in great numbers it may be taken as an almost certain sign of an extra good rise on the part of the fish, and an exceedingly light basket on that of the angler. From an entomo-logical point of view it is a very interesting insect, being, as far as I know, the only member of the Ephemeridæ family which carries the whole of its eggs in a ball in this way; and it has specially lent itself to experimental hatching of the larvæ in captivity, owing to the facility with which the eggs can be taken without injury either to them or to the fly itself. In 1886 we took a very con-siderable number of these eggs. On July 16 we placed them in water on stones. They at once adhered to them. These stones were carefully taken up to London and turned into various vessels in aquaria in the greenhouse of my friend Mr. Hawksley. They were there followed and studied from day to day under the microscope, with the result that the gradual development of the embryo in the egg was noted; and although on many occasions H. began to despond, and to think that

they never would hatch, yet after perseverance, by
February 18, 1887, many of them had hatched out
into larvæ, of which, from our want of knowledge of
the necessities, surroundings, and possibly food, also
possibly from the fact of the London water not suit-
ing them, the majority only survived a few weeks,
and the last ended its existence at the comparatively early age of three months.

It is not a good policy, I think, to be continually
changing fly during the short evening rise. Red
quill, red spinner, detached badger, or occasionally
the jenny spinner, although not so often as the
different forms of red spinner, are, as before indicated, the best patterns. No. 1 Whitchurch used to
be a good pattern of evening fly; lately, however,
it does not seem to have done as well. This, possibly, is because it is not so often fished. In any
case, if these flies are not successful in rising a
particular fish, perhaps the only change worth
making is to a smut; and if, again, that is unsuccessful, go back to one of the previous patterns and
try another fish. Sometimes I have been desperate
myself. I have seen and tried every imaginable
fly—smuts, duns, spinners, sedges—and all to no
purpose, and yet the fish seemed to be rising in
all directions and to be taking everything; and all
I can say is, it is incomprehensible.

I am decidedly of opinion that during the evening rise the fish take better in deep water than
on the shallows; and hence, for preference, level

runs of medium depth should be selected, rather
than shallows on which the fish are often bulging or
tailing, and feeding on larvæ, shrimps, &c., rather
than on fly. When you do hook a fish, kill him as
quickly as possible. There is no time to waste, and
one must remember that, after all, if everything goes
off well—that is to say, if you happen to hit upon
the right fly, the right fish, the right place, the right
moment, and they all *connect*, and you are not
broken—the outside sport that you can achieve cannot by any possibility exceed two brace of good
fish. Remember that if anything goes wrong, it is a
very inconvenient light to repair tackle by.

At the end of the small-fly rise, that is, just at
dusk, no fly is so successful as a small sedge dressed
on a No. o hook, either the silver sedge or an orange
sedge with hare's ear body. Comparatively still
places in deepish water are the best to select. Of
course a fish under your own bank is, as a rule, a far
more likely one than in the middle of the stream or
by the opposite bank, and altogether the fish are not
quite so particular. I think a dry fly is certainly
an advantage, although there are some who are
not particular even on this question. You can get
comparatively close to your fish, and I think the
fault the majority of anglers make is not getting
close enough. If you are very close the under-
handed cast is a decided advantage, because, no
matter how dark it is, in all probability the fish
looking up from the water can discern any moving

o

object above the surface of the water against the sky. As to changing your fly even at this time of evening, or even later, the operation presents no difficulty. If you cannot, by holding the eye of the hook up to the light, get a sufficiently clear view to pass the gut through the eye once, strike a match and do so; and having once got the gut through the eye, if you use Major Turle's knot it does not require sight—it is only a question of feeling to tie it, and hence there can be little difficulty.

We now come to the very last stage, namely, that of fishing with a large sedge when it is almost dark. I am strongly of opinion that this particular class of fishing should be prohibited. It only serves to render the fish, if possible, more shy in the day-time than they are now; it is, as a rule, not to my mind the very finest of sport, because it is only in special circumstances and under special lights that one can see one's fly. I fear, however, that if it were prohibited the number of large fish killed in many of our southern streams would be very largely decreased.

The angler ought to be, if possible, on the eastern bank, looking up into the light towards the portion of the horizon in which the sun has set, except that on moonlight nights he should, for preference, place himself in such a position as to be looking into the moon. In the opposite direction his shadow, being on the water, must certainly scare the fish. Stout gut may be used with advantage. The floating fly is, I think, as necessary as at any

time during the day; and for patterns, all the sedges
are practically good—the large silver or the orange,
or the orange sedge with a hare's ear body, dressed
upon a hook of about No. 2, or the artful dodger,
or Hammond's adopted, or a large Wickham on a
No. 4 hook.

I do not, however, think that the pattern is very
important. If the natural fly is dark, select a dark
one, and if light, a light one. One must not expect
many rises. When you have seen a fish rise in this
light mark down the spot as correctly as possible;
get within ten yards if you can do so, or even nearer
sometimes; throw accurately, do not throw too frequently, and be most particular to dry your fly. Cast
either up or across and partly up the stream, and
above all do not drag your fly. If you are anxious
to fish down-stream, better at once boldly throw off
all pretence of using a floating fly. Put on two big
sedges and flog steadily wet down-stream. In all
cases at the slightest suspicion of a rise strike gently,
but not too quickly, because fish take a large fly
more slowly than a small one; and having hooked
your fish, give no law. Do not be afraid of weedy
places. Trout, as I have said, seldom weed at night,
probably because they do not see the angler, and
grayling very seldom take well as late as this. The
moment you are sure that the fish you are trying is
set down leave him and go on to another. Do not,
above all, waste time, because the rise is a very
short one and very soon over. If you are in doubt

as to whether there is a tangle or a hitch in the gut, run your hand down the cast from the point of your rod to the fly and see that it is all clear. It is not a bad plan to carry a spare cast round your hat with a large sedge attached, because if there is anything of a tangle it is almost impossible to disentangle it at night, and it is an easier plan to take off the old cast and knot on the new one. Of course in changing your fly you will, as mentioned in an earlier part of the chapter, use Major Turle's knot. It certainly is not worth the trouble of changing your fly excepting to vary the size.

One often hears the expression "splashing at sedge" used. Do not believe it. Fish do not splash at sedge. I had long suspected this, but the experience at the end of May 1885 described in a previous chapter, "Studies of Fish Feeding," fully confirmed this suspicion.

Sometimes after a long spell of dry weather a wet night turns out a very good one for this class of fishing. I have vivid recollection of one such on July 21, 1884, when, only starting after half-past seven o'clock at night, I hooked in one meadow six fish, and succeeded in losing five of them in different ways, none of them, however, broken, although the place was very weedy. The only fish I killed was over three pounds, and, curious to say, hooked in the anal fin.

I can recall one evening in 1886 which, to my mind, was so pre-eminently a good one for sedge-fly fishing that I feel tempted to give a little personal experience. It was on July 5, after a hot, dry day, with very little fly and no sport beyond returning a few undersized grayling, that I started out with about the usual anticipation of an evening's sport. I started somewhat late, made the best of my way to the eastern bank of the river, and slowly commenced moving up-stream, looking out for a rise. I was not long in finding one, and the very first cast —which was, to my mind, passing fair and clean —with a detached badger set him down at once. I hence retired, imagining that he would come on the rise in another moment or two. However, I saw no more of him. Walking a few paces up-stream, a similar thing occurred. Changed my fly to a smaller and lighter one; saw another fish rise. Put the fly to him. Again set down; and so on with fish after fish; so that, having walked some distance, and finding myself at a position where there was a convenient bridge to cross the stream and make the best of my way home, I felt that the case was so desperate as to give me every desire to thus beat a retreat. It was very nearly dark; the small-fly rise was over. I had not had a single rise, although trying as well as I knew how fish after fish, and I must confess to having felt somewhat downhearted. I crossed over to the western bank, and walked down slowly, of course peering out into the darkness (and practically it was darkness, being on that side of the river), in hopes of seeing something disturbing the surface. I arrived at length at the upper part of North Head shallow, when for the first time the sound of a rising fish caused me to stop and take a general observation of the state of things. It was still about dusk, and an extraordinary number of sedge flies were moving about in the sedges along the margin of the stream. I stepped down gently close to the bank, and found myself practically surrounded by them, like being in a swarm of bees. I listened, and again I heard the rise. After a time I managed to spot the exact position of it, and kneeling down, judging as well as I could the length of the line, had a cast over him. A very small movement aroused my suspicions, and the next moment I found a good fish careering down the shallow in front of me. Without much hesitation I jumped into the water to get past an awkward stile, and had to take the fish almost down to the bottom of the shallow, when I netted out a nice-looking fish just over two pounds and three-quarters.

After this, feeling somewhat consoled, and having arrived at a portion of the river in which, owing to a bend, looking up-stream placed one in a position where the light was very good, I put up a fresh fly one size larger, dark sedge, and presently saw a quiet rise above me—so small a rise that at once I felt certain it was either a very small fish or one of the wary old customers who frequent that shallow but are not often seen feeding on it in the summer excepting at night. My first cast was a very fair one; the fly landed perhaps two feet above where I had seen the rise; and although there was no moon, looking up into the light as I was, I could see it floating down distinctly. Another small rise, an instinctive strike, and a rush up-stream with the line flying off my reel at such a pace as to make me feel nervous was almost the first indication I had of having hooked a fish. I had to jump into the water again to get round the fence, as the stile is set some distance back, and by the time I got on to the bank immediately above that place, found myself all alone, with no assistant to handle the net, and with a large fish about twenty yards from me just above the head of the island, and apparently with every intention of plunging down on the far side of it from me. I steadied him for a moment or two, and managed to get the better of him to the extent of a few yards. Again he took a few more yards of line, and I was on the point of jumping into the water to follow him to the other side of the island. However, after persevering—he in trying to get on the other side of the island, and I in taking every inch of line I could get—eventually I commenced to get on terms with the fish, and got him gradually near me. In time I got a comparatively short line on the fish, and he then for the first time really showed himself. I had suspected all along that it was not a very small fish, and, I confess, felt nervous when I saw his broad side as he leapt out of the water. However, I had very little time to think, as he was off with a rush again down-stream; so back I stepped into the water, round past the fence end, and ran along as quickly as I could to get below him. Getting below him, and fighting him every inch of the way, and stopping him every moment from plunging into the various beds of weed, I eventually dragged him down to the lower end of the shallow and into the deep water below, where, getting out the net after two or three more or less unsuccessful attempts, I succeeded in guiding him into it, and lifted out a heavy fish. It was too dark to weigh him there and then, but on my way home I met my friend, who asked me what sport I had had. I told him one fish over two and three-quarter pounds, and another good one. To his inquiry, "How big?" I said, "Oh, about four pounds." He said, "Let me see;" and added, "No; that is a very well-conditioned fish, but he will not go four pounds." However, when we got home and weighed him, we found that, although a very short fish, he was in such perfect condition as to turn the scale at, and slightly above, four pounds and nine ounces. This fish, which I believe is as handsome a specimen of a Test trout as has ever been killed, is now the property of the Fly Fisher's Club.

CHAPTER X.

HOOKING, PLAYING, AND LANDING.

ALL the previous chapters written have led up to, and included, the point of rising the fish, and we have now arrived at the stage when, having risen the fish, we must consider what is necessary in order to hook it. Two apparently distinct sets of opinion exist on this subject—one that the policy is to strike, and the other not to strike. I describe these as only *apparently* differences of opinion, because it is a moot question whether both are not in reality one and the same though expressed in different language. The advocates of the striking policy certainly do not mean to advise giving a snatch or a sudden jerk, and hence running a grave risk of breaking the gut and leaving the fly in the fish's mouth. On the other hand, the advocate of the non-striking policy does, in all probability, slightly and slowly raise his hand just to tighten on the fish when it takes. Hence I would suggest that the argument is not only an unprofitable one, but is based on a mutual misconception of each other's meaning. When the rise is seen and the fly is taken, it is necessary to raise the hand and forearm slightly with the object of fixing the barb of the hook firmly in the fish's jaws. I confess I am inclined to call this action *striking*; and if I do so, the non-striking fisherman must not imagine that I am at variance with him, unless he means to argue that no motion of the hand at all is required, and that the fish must either hook himself without any tightening of the line, or that if he fails to do so no action of the fisherman can in any way tend to produce this result.

It must be remembered that there is a very considerable difference in the manner of taking a fly by large or small fish. A small fish comes up to it with a dash, takes it quickly, finds out his mistake quickly, and he ejects the bundle of feathers with which he has been deluded equally quickly. In this case it is necessary to strike at once. A large fish, on the contrary, raises his head leisurely in the water, slowly sucks in the insect floating over him, and quietly turns his head and goes down to swallow the tasty morsel; hence the effect of striking quickly would be either to pull the fly away from him before he gets fairly hold of it, or if he just has it in his mouth, merely to scratch and scare him. It is, of course, difficult for any fisherman to preserve his equanimity at the moment of a large fish taking his fly; but, at the same time, to fail to do so, and in his excitement either to drag the fly away before the trout or grayling has secured it, or to scratch him, is to upset all previous calculations, and at the very moment that success is in his grasp to undo all the work he has previously efficiently performed. A quite appreciable pause should intervene between the moment of a large fish taking and the tightening of the line on the part of the fisherman to hook him ; in fact, as a general rule with fish of one pound or over, it is quite soon enough to strike when the head is turned down. It may very likely be safely inferred that a surprisingly large proportion of the cases of so-called *coming short* are in reality blunders of the angler in his impatience to secure his prey.

Of equal importance with the precise moment when to strike is the further one of the precise degree of force to be employed in striking, and it is astonishing how little is really requisite, and any excess is worse than useless, and only too likely to produce a smash. Of course slack line on the water delays to a small degree the action of striking, and, to a somewhat smaller degree, decreases the force of the blow. One golden rule may be unhesitatingly laid down without fear of contradiction, namely, *strike from the reel*, i.e., do not put your hand on the line so as in any way to hold it when striking, but let the full force of the action of your hand come on the line and on the click of the winch. In this way many a smash is saved and a good fish secured, which would otherwise go away with a sore mouth, and an inclination rather to get rid of the hook in his mouth than to feed again. The resistance of the check in a properly made winch, as before remarked, should be very slight, so that if a trifle too much power has been put into the strike the line comes off the winch, and saves your breaking the gut.

Now, suppose your fish is properly hooked, the very first thing to do is at once to obtain command of it by getting the rod-point well up; this position is technically called *butting* a fish. By this is not understood what the late Francis Francis aptly styled middle-jointing the fish, or raising the rod and placing it inclined backwards over your shoulder, and thus not only running a considerable risk of straining the rod, but, what is even more likely to militate against the ultimate success of killing your fish, practically losing all control over your rod. If your fish should make a sudden rush or a spring into the air with the rod in this position, it is scarcely possible to get the rod-point down quickly enough to save a break, and if he should run in under your feet, you cannot assist your efforts to keep a tight line to the smallest extent by getting the rod-point farther back. When butting the fish the rod should be held at about an angle of sixty degrees with the water-level, and it is only just at the very critical moment of netting the exhausted fish that it should be in a more perpendicular position. When putting the reel on the rod it is a good plan to place it so that its handle is on the left side when the rings are turned downwards, and immediately the fish has been struck the rod should be transferred from the right to the left hand,

and in the act of transferring it be turned over, so that the rings are upwards, and the reel-handle in position for the right hand to control it. The effect of this is to correct the invariable tendency of rods, when much used, to get bowed and set in a curve with the rings on the concave side.

If the first rush of the hooked fish is up-stream, let him go, and do not hold him too hard until turned; if he hangs about in the same place or seems inclined to work down-stream, get below him at once, and in this case, as well as that of the fish who has just been turned from his first mad rush up-stream, drag him down as quickly as you can. Keep well below him on a short line, and keep dragging him down for some distance; in fact, as a golden rule, *use your heels to save your reel.* In this way you keep on taking him farther and farther from his home into a strange country, where every obstacle, weed, post, or pile, is unknown to him, and hence he is unable to entangle you in them with that degree of decision and certainty he can exercise when close to home. In addition to this, you are every moment taking more out of him in the most efficacious way, and rapidly drowning him, as it is called.

It seems anomalous to speak of drowning a fish in his native element, yet it is not altogether an inappropriate expression, as the coroner's verdict in such a case would be "death by suffocation." A fish requires for breathing purposes to take in water through his mouth and eject it through his gills, in

which action the oxygen required for breathing is
extracted by the aid of the special apparatus contained in the gills for that purpose called *branchiæ*.
When the fish's head is directed up-stream, the
natural flow of the water assists him greatly in this
function of nature, but the moment his head is
turned down-stream the process is partially reversed,
the water passing *in* at the gills and *out* of the
mouth whenever he opens them to breathe, causing an insufficient supply of the necessary oxygen
and consequent suffocation; hence the great and
manifest advantage of pulling him down with the
current, and the faster the stream the more rapid
its action.

While playing a fish, as full a strain as the rod and
tackle will conveniently bear should be kept steadily
on him, and it would probably astonish even the
most experienced anglers to measure how little force
this really represents. Very few full-sized salmon-
rods can lift a dead weight of two pounds, and an
ordinary single-handed trout-rod probably cannot
exert a greater pressure than, say, half a pound, or at
most three-quarters of a pound, when playing a fish.
With large fish the best policy is to put on as much
strain as possible at once. A large proportion of
lost fish owe their escape to getting out of control by a want of prompt decision when first playing
them; and with a very lightly hooked fish, perhaps,
all things considered, it is as well to lose him at
once rather than a few moments later. A lively,

active trout of about one pound and a half will not, however, without getting unhooked, bear the same strain as a large one; and hence with fish of this size and character much judgment can be shown by the angler who has *good hands* on his fish when to hold him and when to ease him.

If all is smooth sailing, or, in other words, if your fish does not succeed in getting into weeds or winding the line round a post, &c.—and you can, to a great degree, prevent this by keeping his head well on top of the water—there is no great difficulty in killing the very largest fish. If he jumps, and as often as he jumps, at once lower the point of the rod until he is back in the water, to prevent the full momentum of his falling weight coming on your tackle. As soon as he is back in the water the rod should again be placed at an angle of sixty degrees.

Sometimes all efforts to keep his head up and prevent his burying himself in a bed of weeds are unavailing; and here one of the most difficult positions occurs for the angler. If it is in quite shallow water, the fisherman can generally wade in and, keeping a steady strain, walk up or down to the place, and thus either scare the fish out, or if he will, as Uncle Remus styles it, "lie low," occasionally he can be extracted by the landing-net. If at the first rush he simply makes a straight dive into and through the weeds, he generally breaks you at once. If when first hooked you can foresee this probability, the best plan is not to hold him, but

let him run to weed, and take the risk of getting
him out afterwards.

When a fish is once weeded, the following tactics
are what I should suggest :—Firstly, get well below
the fish, lower the point of the rod so as to take all
strain off it, and keep a slight steady pressure on the
line. If after a few minutes the fish does not stir,
let out plenty of line, and take hold of the line with
the hand clear of the rod-point, and draw steadily,
sawing lightly, still holding the rod in the other hand
in case the fish should make a sudden rush. I would
caution my readers that the strain to be put on the
fish must be a very slight one. If the effect of this
pressure is to move the fish, let go the line at
once, and again restore the pressure from the rod-
point. If this plan of pulling the line by hand is
unsuccessful, draw plenty of the line off the reel and
slack the fish altogether, even, if you like, laying the
rod down and waiting some minutes. This plan of
slacking altogether is often most efficacious and far
more successful than many of my readers would
imagine. The moment the fish moves, the line
running through the water will give timely warning
and enable you once more to resume your rod and
play the fish. If still unsuccessful one more chance
remains, and that is, to cut away the weed around
the fish with a sharp implement fixed on a handle.

The cutting instrument usually made by tackle-
makers, and called, I think, the "Angler's Friend,"
is one of the best for the purpose. It is, however,

a desperate and last resource, and even with the greatest care there is considerable risk of cutting the line. If all the above methods, after being tried one after the other, prove unavailing, you must, I fear, bear with equanimity the loss of your fish, or rather what might have been your fish. You have had a varied entertainment, and have tried in succession all the dodges I know to get him out of his strong position, and your only resource now is to raise the siege. Very often if you do so, and manage to draw your line out of the weeds, you will find that the trout has by this time saved you any anxiety by himself effecting a fracture of the gut next to the hook.

If a fish is hooked in a place with very heavy banks of weed, he can, as a general rule, be prevented from hanging you up by a somewhat summary process, which, however, must be adopted almost immediately after he is hooked. The moment your fish is held in such a position, put on a strong strain and get his head well up alongside the bank of weeds, or even on it, keep your eye on the fish, and once having got his head up, never let him get it down again. Each time he tries to do so take a couple of turns of your reel-handle, the effect of which will be to draw his head up again, and the more he struggles the more quickly he propels himself on the top of the weeds towards you. It is quite astonishing how fish after fish can at times be killed in such a place by resolutely and immediately following these tactics.

P

Though at night a trout does not often weed, if he does at any rate he does not weed deeply, and this is probably due to the angler not being easily seen; and in the same way in daylight, if the fisherman keeps well out of sight of a hooked fish, he can often be killed in the midst of heavy weeds without once attempting to get into them. Grayling do not as a rule go to weed as often or as resolutely as trout, and scarcely ever really entangle the tackle in it; so that if a grayling does go to weeds, by waiting with a moderately tight line he can generally be persuaded out of them. A fish hooked above a bridge or a hatch will probably on his first rush make a bolt down, and even occasionally through; but, as before noted, in the case of the bridge they usually only run down under it, and do not go through, but remain in the shade beneath the bridge. In such a case too much strain should not be put on when running down, but a steady and severe strain maintained when the fish is under the bridge will usually in time bring him up again. If the bridge is a narrow one, or in the case of a hatch, the rod may be passed through and the fish killed at leisure below.

Sometimes a fish running up or down, but more often down, towards a dangerous spot may be turned by the angler getting in front of him and pulling him *towards* the place of danger, which the fisherman wants him to avoid. Owing to his natural *contrairiness*, he will often turn and go in the opposite direction, and when once clear of danger it is as well, if possible, not to let him get back to it.

As long as the angler is playing a fish he should try to keep a uniform strain on the rod, and by no means let it get slack. He can usually avoid putting on too much strain by looking at the curve made by the bowed rod, if necessary easing to it a trifle. A fish hooked at the end of a long line at the moment he feels the hook will sometimes run straight in under your feet, and then it is impossible to get in your line fast enough to avoid slacking. If this should happen do not be in a hurry or flurry; if the fish was lightly hooked he is gone; and if, on the other hand, the barb is fairly home, he will simply go down in the weeds, or near the bottom of the river and sulk. Meanwhile you can leisurely reel in your line, and proceed to play the fish as soon as it is taut again.

An uncomfortable feeling is produced when a hooked fish indulges in what is called *jiggering;* this expression means a series of quick short jerky pulls followed by an equally quick slacking of the line. If the fish is visible you will notice that he is going through a curious set of antics, wriggling about and doubling himself up in a strange way. How to account for it I do not know. Perhaps salmon are more given to it than trout or grayling. Some angling authorities have said that it is a lightly hooked fish; but, if allowed to judge from my own experience, I cannot recall many instances of having lost jiggering fish. Altogether, however, it does make one feel nervous and uncomfortable.

Sometimes a fish seems to dive in under your own bank, or to be trying to find his way into rat-holes or under a ledge. In such a case the reason of his tactics is to try and fray the tackle against the ledge or other projection, and it is necessary for the angler to keep his rod in a horizontal position, with a good strain on the fish. Some years ago a very curious instance of a somewhat similar occurrence happened to me when fishing a small Hertfordshire stream. I had hooked an undoubtedly good-sized fish; he at once ran in under my own bank, and, to my astonishment, continued running line off the reel. Naturally I imagined that he had run round a post and was back in the stream. With a view of disentangling the line from it, I stepped up to the place, when I found at right angles to the course of the stream a large drain-pipe, up which my fish had bolted, it probably being his usual hiding-place when not feeding. Keeping the rod in a horizontal position, and standing immediately over the mouth of the pipe, I continued playing this fish, my chief, in fact my only care being to prevent the line from coming in contact with any portion of the circumference of the pipe. This performance lasted some minutes; to me it seemed some hours; and at length inch by inch I recovered line, and eventually had the satisfaction of landing a four-pound trout in perfect condition. This happened in the morning, and, strange to say, the only other fish I killed .that day was a three-pound fish hooked at the same place in the evening, who pursued precisely the same tactics, and eventually succumbed to precisely the same treatment.

Now having tired your fish, keeping still below him, place the landing-net in the water below him, and always hold the net in the lower hand; that is to say, if you are on the right-hand bank looking up-stream, in the left hand; and if you are on the left-hand bank, in the right. The position of an angler just on the point of landing a trout is illustrated in the frontispiece, which is an accurate reproduction of an instantaneous photograph taken on the Test by Messrs. Elliott & Fry. Keep the net still and well sunk, and judging the length of the line accurately to bring the fish to the net, draw him down and drop him into the net. Remember that the test of a fish being ready for the net is his turning on his side. When the fish is in the net do not lift it, but draw it to the bank; take the fish out of the net; if he is undersized unhook him gently and return him to the water. Do not dash him down and kill him, but drop him quietly; and if you find he is sick and disposed to turn on his side or back, nurse him, hold him in his proper position with his head up-stream, in a place where the stream is not too strong, and in ninety-nine out of a hundred cases he will in a few minutes recover and swim away. If he is sizeable knock him on the head to put him out of pain, and remember that one smart blow on the right spot is sufficient. The right spot is exactly at the summit. of the spinal column where the head joins the body. Straighten him out, lay him in your basket on dry rushes or grass or nettle, or in a linen bag or wrapped up in a towel. As soon as he is stiff, if you want him to look well, close his mouth and bend him down bellywards to hog his back, as this always makes fish look more shapely.

CHAPTER XI.

AUTOPSY.

ONE of the first objects of a true sportsman should be to study and observe the habits and habitat of his quarry, so as to acquire an intimate knowledge of the class of food most affected by it and best calculated to sustain and improve its condition. With respect to birds preserved and even bred entirely for sporting purposes, a very considerable amount of attention has been paid to this branch of the subject ; and considering the paramount importance of this point to the fly-fisherman, whose only lure is an imitation of the fish's natural food, it is surprising how persistently he deludes himself and others by neglect of the simplest plan of observation, viz., that of examining the contents of the trout or grayling's stomach, and thus ascertaining for an absolute fact the nature of the meal on which his appetite has been assuaged. The continual complaint of not being able to discover the species of insect on which the fish are feeding, or, worse still, the confident tone in which one is assured that the angler could see the trout taking iron-blue or olive duns, and yet could not persuade them to look at

the very best imitation, becomes tedious from its
frequent reiteration. Yet to the large number of
grumblers who indulge in these vain laments it
never seems to occur that, providing only they can
succeed in catching a feeding fish—not always a very
easy feat to accomplish—the remedy is in their own
hands, and a few moments devoted to a careful
autopsy will at once solve the problem.

Having caught your fish, and given him a smart
tap on the head to kill him, hold him in the left
hand with back downwards, and with a sharp knife,
inserted at the vent, edge upwards, so as not to cut
into the entrails, make one incision right up to
the gills. Turn the flanks outwards, and pull the
whole of the internal arrangements upwards and
clear of the fish, except, of course, just at the throat,
where a clean cut is required to sever the tube, and
thus separate the entrails from the remainder of the
fish. Plate XXI. is a longitudinal section of a
trout, showing the digestive organs, air bladder,
pyloric appendages, &c. A portion of the stomach
is cut open to show the undigested food it contains.
The tube leading from the stomach to the vent, which
contains only digested food, can be discarded. Commencing at the gullet end, the throat and stomach
should be slit down longitudinally, and the contents
carefully turned out into a small vessel containing
water. Perhaps, if the fish are rising very freely,
many anglers will think they would never have the
patience to perform this operation deliberately. It

PLATE XXI.

AUTOPSY.

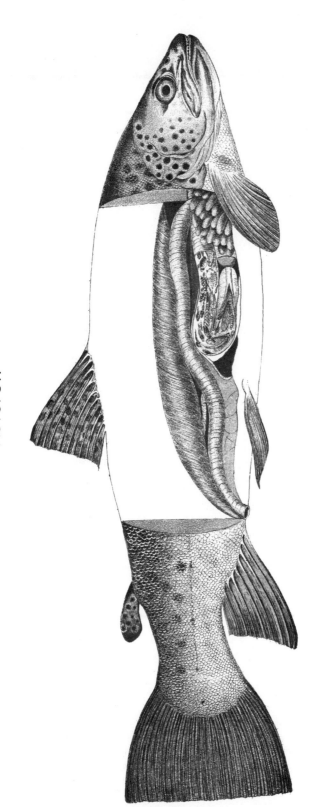

TROUT (*Salmo fario*)

Leighton Brothers, *Lith.*

E. Kemp. del.

certainly is not a waste of time to do so; but one's
sympathy must be with the ardent sportsman, who,
having secured one, burns to achieve the further
distinction of making it a brace. But if you cannot
have the patience, there is often an easy way of
getting a part of the information you require by
opening the mouth of the fish and taking from it on
the point of a knife a few of the last insects he has
seized but not yet swallowed. Turning these into
a vessel of water, and examining through an ordinary
magnifying-glass will, after some little experience
and study, tell the fisherman something about the
insects, or at least show him to which family they
belong, and in which stage they are being taken by
the fish.

However, to return to the contents of the vessel
into which the whole of the undigested food has
been turned. The first thing that will strike the
observant student is, that one portion of the food
is lighter than water, and therefore floating on the
surface, but that a far larger proportion is of greater
specific gravity, and hence sinks to the bottom. The
floating portion consists of winged insects and
nymphæ just on the point of assuming the winged
state. It may fairly be asked how this last fact is
ascertained, and any one taking the trouble can
easily prove the question to his own satisfaction.
Let him take two or three of the floating nymphæ,
and as many of the sunk ones, and soak them for a
few minutes in water in which is dissolved a small

piece of ordinary washing soda. This is necessary
to counteract the action of the digestive fluid of the
fish, which is strongly acid, and if neglected, digestion or decomposition will continue for some time.
After washing thoroughly in water to free from soda,
these nymphæ may be dropped into a small bottle
with methylated spirit, and kept for almost any
length of time without apparent change. To make
them sufficiently transparent for a thorough examination under the microscope, they should be immersed
for some days in oil of cloves. When transparent
they should be placed on a glass slip on the stage of
the microscope under a low-power objective, such as
3 ins. or $1\frac{1}{2}$ in., which are equivalent to magnifying
powers respectively of about 15 and 30. A great
contrast will be at once apparent between those that
floated and those that sank. In every one that
floated it will be seen that inside the setæ or tails
of the nymph are plainly visible the setæ of the
sub-imago, which is just about emerging from it ; and
in the same way, in each of the six legs, in the head,
in each antenna, and even in the abdomen itself,
the distinct outline, with every detail of the corresponding limb or organ of the sub-imago, may be
seen.

In fact, in general appearance, the nymph consists
of two distinct portions, the inner or solid-looking
portion being the sub-imago complete in all its parts
excepting that the wings are folded up inside a pair
of somewhat oval-shaped covers ; this sub-imago is,

however, entirely enveloped in a thin transparent covering, which is perceptibly larger than, and projects beyond the outline of, the insect itself. Attached to this apparently loose covering are all the organs which are especially provided for the larva living in the water, and not required for its subsequent or winged stage, and these organs are, without exception, shed with the larval envelope. Among these the most prominent are the various mouth organs, and the *branchiæ*, or external portion of the breathing apparatus. The less developed nymphæ, which sank in the water when the autopsy was originally performed, have, however, quite a different appearance. There is little or no appearance of the larval covering being loose ; the setæ and legs are solid-looking limbs, the latter often armed with formidable claws ; the mandibles and other mouth organs are very prominent, and firmly attached to the head ; in fact, there is no indication of an impending metamorphosis. In considering the deduction to be drawn from the comparison between the proportionate quantity of sunk and floating nymphæ from the autopsy, it must be remembered that all of the floating specimens were nymphæ rising to the surface for the purpose of emerging from the envelope in the sub-imago state, and hence were taken in mid-water, while the sunk ones were down among the weeds or on the gravel, and must be considered as *bottom* food.

The remainder of the floating portion of the

autopsy will, at the first glance, be thought to
consist entirely of winged insects. Some are, in
fact, so, among which must be classed *curses* or
little black midges of all sorts, winged ants, any of
the winged Phryganidæ, and a portion of the residue,
which at a superficial examination will all look like
winged Ephemeridæ. Such of these as are in the
imago state are easy to separate, and, of course,
represent floating flies taken by the fish; but of the
duns or Ephemeridæ in the sub-imago stage, it will
be found, by careful microscopic examination, that a
considerable proportion have their wings still folded
up along the longitudinal nerving; but the trans-
verse folding has become extended, owing to fracture
or decomposition of the wing-covers. A further
examination will in these often bring out the fact
that the abdomen is still enveloped in the larval
shuck with the *branchiæ* attached. Hence it may
be inferred that these, again, when taken by the fish
were nymphæ, and were not on the surface of the
water. In fact, the tendency of careful scrutiny of
the contents of the stomachs of both trout and
grayling is tending in one direction, viz., that of
showing how small a proportion of the fish's insect
food is taken when floating, and how large a proportion belongs to the middle and lower depths of
the stream.

Considerable space has here been devoted to the
smaller or floating portion of our original autopsy,
as this is essentially the part requiring study by the

votary of the dry fly. A brief outline of the probable composition of the solid mass of sunk animal matter, forming by far the greater portion of every autopsy, will not be out of place. Apart from small, semi-digested or detached pieces, the predominating larvæ found in stomachs of fish killed in chalk-streams are those of the smaller and medium-sized Ephemeridæ, both in the early or larva stage and in that of the nympha—a nympha being simply a larva in which the development of the wing-covers has sufficiently advanced to be visible under the magnifying-glass or microscope. As before remarked, the nymph immediately before the metamorphosis to the sub-imago is not found among the sunk portion of the autopsy.

The immature larvæ of the May-fly, living in burrows excavated in the mud, are, as might be expected, rarely found in the fish's stomach. I have never discovered any of the *flat* larvæ of Ephemeridæ in either trout or grayling. These are the immature forms of the genera Ecdyurus and Heptagenia, of which the March Brown and Yellow May Dun are the best known British species. They live on the under side of stones in swift shallow water. They adhere so closely to the stones, and, after covering themselves with sand or other fine detritus, are so like them in colour, that it is questionable whether the fish would notice them at all; and if they did, it is even more questionable whether they could detach them from the stones. As a general rule, a considerable number of shrimps are present, as well as a few caddis in their cases, stones which are probably the undigested residuum of other caddis-cases, often snails, and occasionally beetles of various kinds.

Plate XXII. is a reproduction from microscopic drawings taken from life, in which 1, 2, and 3 are Ephemeridæ—1 and 2 immature nymphs, and 3 another nymph just on the point of changing to the sub-imago state; 4 is the fresh-water shrimp (*Gammarus pulex*), and 5 and 6 are *caddis* or larvæ of Phryganidæ with their cases.   On Plate XXIII. the nymphæ are shown magnified three diameters, and on Plate XXIV. the shrimp, caddis, and cases magnified to the same degree.   Sometimes there are a few larvæ of the smaller Perlidæ, and very rarely in the Test minnows or bullheads.   During the autumn grains of corn are frequently found in grayling, but not, as far as my personal experience goes, in trout, and, perhaps, altogether, the contents of the grayling's stomach may be briefly described as more heterogeneous than that of the trout.

From a scientific point of view, it is certainly desirable that fly fishermen should prosecute steadily from day to day, and from season to season, the study of autopsy, but at the same time it will be of very little use to them unless they will well and truly " mark, learn, and inwardly digest " the results of their study, and, by careful reasoning, work out for themselves the ultimate teaching, so that it will tend to assist them in the difficult problem of selecting the most likely pattern of fly, especially with shy fish who are not

PLATE XXII.

AUTOPSY.

Baetis
Nymph

1

Ephemerella ignita
Nymph

2

Baetis
Nymph

3

Shrimp
(*Gammarus pulex*)

4

Caddis

Larva Case
5

Caddis

Larva Case
6

infrequently either killed or set down altogether by
the very first cast.

It has been already shown that by far the larger
proportion of the contents of the stomach of a trout or
grayling consists of larvæ, nymphæ, caddis, shrimps,
&c., which are invariably in the middle and lower
depths of the water, from which fact the inference
must be drawn that the major part of their food
is taken below the surface. At the first glance, a
natural deduction from this would be, that the sunk
fly would be more likely to tempt than the floating
one. Very possibly many of the sparely dressed patterns used more generally in the north for wet-fly
fishing are taken for some forms of larvæ, or even in
some cases water-beetles, and it has been confidently
said by north country anglers of great experience,
that an adept of their style could work sad havoc
on some of the well-stocked shallows of the chalk-
streams. Unfortunately very few of the disciples of
the dry fly practise, even if they understand, the art of
fishing with sunk fly, which may account for the fact
that as a general rule when tried in the Hampshire
streams it has not proved successful. It would be
well for a first-rate performer to pay a visit to the
Test or Itchen and thoroughly thrash out the point.
It must not be in private water where the trout are
unsophisticated, and when on the feed take anything
looking like an insect, but on one of the well-whipped
waters of the Test or Itchen—such as Houghton on
the former, or the Old Barge at Winchester on the

latter. I confess to feeling very grave doubts as to
the result. If it is to be judged by any attempts
heard of up to the present time, it is foredoomed;
if, on the other hand, previous failures have been due
to want of knowledge or experience on the part of
the fishermen, it is quite on the cards that it might
revolutionise the whole art of fly-fishing as practised in Hampshire. If, however, as I am inclined
to predict, this should be a *fiasco*, the natural question is, to inquire whether it is possible to take
these wary fish when feeding under water with
an imitation of their natural food. The larva has
been frequently imitated, and has occasionally done
well; but, strange to relate, on the days when it
has done well it has almost invariably turned out
that other fishermen on the same waters have also
done well with the dry fly. It has generally been
in the early spring, when the trout are comparatively
easy to catch, and no one would seriously advise the
use of a sunk fly on a day when the floating would
kill as well. At other times of the year there is no
record of the sunk fly having had any chance on such
waters as the above, and occasionally the dry fly is
certainly somewhat efficacious. In any case it must
be remembered that the presence in an autopsy of
nymphæ just on the point of changing to the winged
state indicates that the fish, although, as a rule,
under such conditions looking downwards, has yet
followed the active nymphæ towards the surface; and
if one of them should succeed in reaching the surface

and, splitting open the larval shuck, struggle out
into the winged state, it is not unlikely that the trout
or grayling would seize and swallow it; and if perchance at this moment the angler's very best imitation on invisible gossamer gut should be floating
down towards his nose lightly cocked and sailing
jauntily along, it is also not unlikely that the two
birds will be killed with one stone, or, if all goes
right, a good fish added to those already in the
basket.

Autopsy shows that the diet of grayling is more
various than that of trout. This may, to a certain
extent, account for grayling being, as a rule, less
difficult to catch than trout. In addition to grains
of wheat and oats, it is not uncommon to find a
number of different sorts of water-beetles, insects
looking like large house-flies, cowdung flies, and
many other forms in both larval and perfect stages,
besides, of course, the usual number of larvæ and
nymphæ of the smaller Ephemeridæ, shrimps, &c., in
the capacious paunch of a single grayling. This
seems to indicate a love of a meal in many courses,
or possibly a sort of feminine curiosity, and to this
cause may be attributed the success of many fancy
patterns, such as red tags, orange tags, green insects,
coch-y-bonddhu, bumbles, Wickhams, &c., with
Salmo thymallus. Generally speaking, it may serve
to encourage the fisherman to persevere with a
feeding grayling, and try pattern after pattern, no
matter how unlike anything he may see on the sur-

Q

face of the stream, in hopes of at length chancing
on some combination of feathers, tinsel, and silk
which will tempt the fish to rise and take the glittering object in its mouth, without any suspicion of
the barbed sting lurking unseen under the folds of
the hackle.

Above all, the study of autopsy should teach one
lesson, viz., that the precise shade or tint of the artificial and the exact imitation of the natural fly most
plentiful on the water are not so all-important as
many fly-fishermen seem to imagine. The contents
of the stomach of a fish almost invariably comprise
many different species of the same genus, or many
varieties of the same species. Insects belonging
to different families, or even different orders, are
often side by side. The larvæ and nymphæ closely
packed together in the gullet and stomach are,
when separated and examined with a magnifying-
glass, found to differ in colour from the palest
primrose to the deepest olive, from a light buff
to a deep chocolate-brown. Some are so small
as to be scarcely visible to the naked eye, others
are nearly three-quarters of an inch in length.
Some are in the most rudimentary condition, and
others again are just about to undergo the metamorphosis to the sub-imago and change from a grub
living in the water to a winged insect. Now if fish
feeding, as they do, almost continuously will take
all and every one of these insects, no matter what
colour or in which stage, no matter whether small

PLATE XXIII.

AUTOPSY.

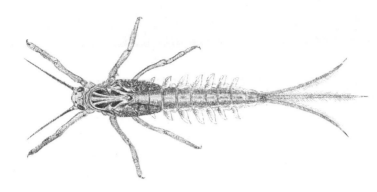

Baetis-Nymph × 3.

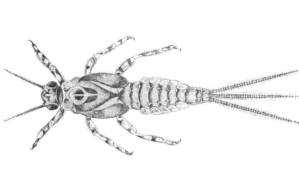

Ehemerella ignita-Nymph × 3.

Baetis-Nymph × 3.

E Kemp. del.

Leighton Brothers, *Lith.*

or comparatively large — Ephemeridæ, Phryganidæ, Diptera, Perlidæ, Sialidæ, as well as Gammari and other Crustacea—it cannot be so much the question of what fly or which pattern is offered to them.

Reasoning from this point, what is the secret of fish in some rivers being so difficult to tempt? The logical deduction seems to be, that a combination of very bright clear water and frequent flogging must be one cause, and probably the presence of a very great quantity and variety of suitable food in the river, as tending to enable the fish to satisfy their appetites with very little exertion, is another cause tending to render them particular, and not easy to beguile with any artificial, no matter how good an imitation of the natural insect.

To carry the reasoning a little further: What, then, must the angler learn and attempt if he wishes to achieve any success in a difficult water? The longer one lives and the more the subject is studied, the more forcibly are the lessons impressed upon one's mind. The fish being frequently cast over get to know the appearance of gut, and to be suspicious of all flies—sometimes even the natural ones; hence the finest gut which will hold the trout or grayling must be used, and the greatest care taken that the artificial fly is placed on the water lightly, that it is perfectly dry and cocked, that it is so placed on the stream as to float down without the smallest semblance of drag or check, following precisely the natural run of the current; and in addition to all of these points, one, and perhaps the most important, is, that all the above conditions should be fulfilled in the very first cast, and before the shyest fish can have the slightest suspicion that he is being deluded. This sentence has in substance been written many times before in this book, but it is so essentially the most important factor in determining the success or want of success of the angler, that no apology is needed for its reiteration. It should be impressed over and over again on the mind of every dry-fly fisherman; in fact, he might be tempted to say, in the immortal words of Molière, though very differently applied by him, " Je les veux faire graver en lettres d'or sur la cheminée de ma salle."

The experience of any angler who has perse-vered in the practical study of the food affected by trout and grayling must tend to prove that when thoroughly on the feed they are not over nice or particular in their choice, and are, like their human congeners, fond of change and variety. Some of the forms of animal life found may be fairly de-scribed in the above words, and, besides, the eloquent lessons taught as to the habits of the fish, must prove of considerable interest, not only as mere ento-mological specimens, but also as conveying a faint idea of the marvellous numbers and sorts of larvæ, beetles, crustacea, &c., living in the water.

In a previous chapter a somewhat curious, though certainly not unique, result of an autopsy was re-ferred to. In this case, one evening at the end of

May, the fish were apparently rising furiously and
splashing heavily, and yet the only one killed had
been regaling himself chiefly on water-snails, or
Limnææ. Any one fishing that evening would, judging from the ordinary dicta of writers on the subject,
have been certain that they were taking some large
fly of the Phryganidæ family, and kept on changing
one sort of sedge fly for another, probably trying
larger and larger patterns, until at last he arrived at
some monstrosity about the size of a grilse fly. If he
had by any chance succeeded in rising, hooking, or
killing a fish with any particular pattern, he would
have been convinced that it was the pattern, colour,
or size which had achieved this success ; whereas
an examination of the contents of the stomach would
have entirely dissipated this notion, and shown him
that it was, after all, an accident, brought about by a
passing humour of the trout or the chance circumstance of the fly floating close to his nose just at the
moment that he was following his intended prey
towards the surface.

In July 1886 Mr. Marryat and I were wandering
rather than fishing in the middle of a hot calm afternoon, when we noticed a fish come to the surface
and take some small insect. This was repeated
several times, not exactly at one spot, but over an
area of perhaps two or three square yards. The rise
was too deliberate for either smutting or bulging, and
yet did not look as if the fish was taking duns or
spinners, of which, by the way, there were very few on

the water. A cinnamon quill on a ooo hook tempted
the fish—a good one nearly 2 lbs.—at the first cast, and
setting to work immediately after landing the trout,
we proceeded to make an autopsy. Of undigested
food there was not much, and what there was consisted of, say, thirty to forty specimens of one and
the same species. It was a small water-beetle with
very short and broad head and beautiful purple
eyes. The elytra or wing-cover was artistically
marbled in a deep purple colour on a neutral ground.
Under these was a pair of very fine and almost transparent flying-wings. The hind-legs were fringed
with hairs all over, and in the lowest joints these
hairs were spread out into a perfect paddle. Fortunately, Mr. Marryat knew the insect at once as one
of the Corixæ, a small water-beetle about a quarter
of an inch in length, which remains under water for
a time, but has to come to the surface occasionally
for air, and can fly as well as swim. This creature
had never before been found by me in an autopsy,
and, strange to relate, since that date I have only
found it on one occasion, and that during the summer
of 1887 in a trout about 3 lbs. caught in the same
part of the same shallow. The insect is not altogether uncommon, and has been found in other parts
of the same water.

Fishing one evening in the early autumn of the
same year in another part of this stream, when there
was a very fine show of the sherry spinner, the
metamorphosis of the blue-winged olive (*Ephe-*

PLATE XXIV.

AUTOPSY.

CADDIS.

Larva × 3.   Case × 3.

CADDIS.

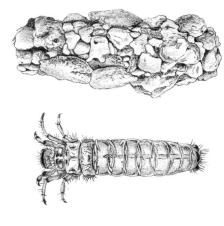

Larva × 3.   Case × 3.

Shrimp (*Gammarus pulex*) × 3.

E.Kemp. del.

Leighton Brothers. *Lith.*

merella ignita of Eaton), a fish was noticed feeding
freely at the lower end of a deep hole, just where
the stream began to flow rapidly. Naturally the
first fly to try was a pale-coloured detached badger,
followed by various patterns of red and ginger quills,
none of which procured any response. A short rest
and a change to a hare's-ear-bodied orange sedge
was successful in deluding him, and after a sharp
but determined fight a handsome trout of 3 lbs.
2 ozs. was safely in the landing-net.

Following the maxim of never attempting to make
an autopsy in the dark, we waited until we arrived
home. The fish was in perfect condition and colour,
and his belly abnormally full. In his mouth and
all the way down his gullet was a compact mass
of sherry spinners, and even after extracting this
the lower portion of the stomach seemed much dis
tended. Careful manipulation then extracted partially digested remains of five fully-grown crayfish,
the largest of which would, when extended, have
measured fully four inches in length. Just imagine
the powers of digestion of a trout to dissolve not
only the interior soft portion but the hard calcareous
shell of these crustacea. Besides, only consider the
appetite of a fish able and willing to take thousands
of sherry spinners with this mass of undigested food
in his capacious maw. Is it surprising that with a
plentiful supply of food they grow so rapidly and
reach such major proportions ?

In an autopsy of a trout last spring I found a

small quantity of weed, and as this was the first
time I ever found free vegetable matter in a trout's
stomach it was only natural to make a microscopic
examination. The weed contained a considerable
number of small caddis enclosed in cases formed of
pieces of rush. It is to be inferred that neither
the weed nor the vegetable case of the caddis was
taken as food by the fish, but that in its attempts
to secure the succulent grub it had to include these
unconsidered trifles.

Grayling fishing last October on a fine and genial
day, after killing two brace of good fish—6¾ lbs.—
with a Wickham, I happened to notice a rise in a deep
hole just inside a swift run. The Wickham, which
had killed previously, landed right at the first
attempt, and the fish rose slowly and steadily, was
fairly hooked, and in the very first dash succeeded
in breaking the fine-drawn gut at a weak place.
After a few minutes (perhaps twenty) had been
occupied in making the necessary repairs to the
tackle, and before knotting on a fresh fly, a quiet
rise in the run about four to five yards above the
place where the fish had been hooked attracted
my notice. It looked very like smutting, as there
did not seem to be any quantity of fly visible on the
water, yet every few minutes another quiet rise was
to be seen at the same spot. Selecting a female
black gnat on a oo hook, and fishing with caution, casting only occasionally once or twice, and
then resting the fish altogether for some minutes, I

persevered, especially as no other feeding fish was
visible. At length he made a mistake, and was duly
killed—a grayling, 2 lbs. 14 ozs. Immediately sus-
pecting that it was the fish who had broken away
just before, a search was instituted to discover
either the Wickham or the mark of the hook, but
neither could be discerned. A considerable number
of willow flies in his mouth, however, tempted me
to make a careful autopsy on our return in the evening, especially as this member of the Perlidæ family
is very seldom found in Test grayling. The whole
of the stomach, gullet, &c., being taken out, cut
away below the gills and slit down, a heavy mass of
willow flies were turned into a saucer of water, and
with a spatula I commenced selecting a few of the
best specimens for preservation. The spatula struck
against something hard in the saucer, and the Wickham was there and then taken out of the water and
dried, to be preserved with the remainder of the
contents of the stomach. This was evidently the very
grayling which had previously broken me. All the
time he was taking the natural willows; yet he rose
at and took a Wickham, was hooked, broken, and
within a short time met his end with a black gnat.
Strangest of all to relate, however, is, that he must
have swallowed the Wickham and hook *after* he
had broken away, for the internal parts of the fish
had been taken out from the belly and the gullet cut
off below the gills.

What a strange answer to the charge of cruelty

brought against fishermen, that a fish should succeed in unhooking himself, then swallow the hook, and a few minutes later take and fall a victim to another artificial, and this one in no way resembling the natural fly on which he had been continuously feeding!

CHAPTER XII.

TROUT OR GRAYLING.

REFERRING to the question of which I propose to treat in this chapter, namely, that of attempting to guide the angler in discriminating from the appearance of the rise or from its position whether the fish is likely to be a trout or a grayling, I must premise by dealing with two very conflicting opinions. Some authorities are strongly opposed to the introduction of grayling into trout streams. Many first-class fishermen say that they do not care for grayling fishing, possibly because they have never really tried it, or equally possibly because they are not quite— I will not say straightforward—but disingenuous and candid in the opinion they are giving. Then they quote Cotton, who wrote that extraordinary sentence about the grayling being the deadest-hearted fish that swims. Cotton certainly never killed a three-pound grayling on a Test shallow; if he had, with his power of discrimination and strong desire for truth, he could not have written that sentence. Some fishermen have even been heard to say that they wished the last pike in the Test might be choked in the act of swallowing the last grayling. This, however smart it may sound, is childish and selfish, as many fishermen consider that grayling fishing is quite as good in its way as the trout, and with these I wish to be numbered.

A grayling of equal weight is a more difficult fish to kill when once hooked than the trout. With the single exception that it very seldom weeds you with that pertinacity exercised by the trout, he tries the tackle more and is more often lost than the trout, unless he is hooked in the leathery ring forming the outer margin of his mouth, in which case the hold is better than any part of the trout. Even if hooked there grayling have a nasty habit, if they can once get below the angler, of boring down-stream and hanging the whole of their weight on the line, and hence as soon as they are hooked it is more essential even to get below them than it is with the trout. When they catch sight of the fisherman their rush is as brilliant and as prolonged as that of any trout.

As regards the difficulty of distinguishing between the rise of a trout and of a grayling, it is no doubt very great as to the rise, *per se*, unless a glimpse can be caught of the dorsal fin of the grayling, which is a very prominent feature. With regard to tailing fish, it is scarcely possible to tell whether it is trout or grayling unless very close, and considering the marked difference in shape between the forked tail of a grayling and the straight or slightly convex one of the trout, this is somewhat surprising. The tail of a grayling is, I think, lighter and more silvery, although distinctly tinged with yellow, than that of the trout, which always appears to me a sort of dark brown hue when standing out of the water.

In attempting to distinguish trout from grayling when rising, the main difference is certainly the position of the rise rather than the nature of it—its position, I mean, with regard to the character of the water and the time of the year, modified by the fact that, as a general rule, it may be taken that grayling are less prone to rise quite close to the bank than are trout. In the early spring, before the trout have got thoroughly fixed in their positions, and are rising more or less all over the stream, when the grayling, just having spawned, are also feeding, it is difficult to be certain which is rising, and the best judges are often mistaken, whether it be on a shallow or on a smooth glide above a shallow, or anywhere, in fact, excepting deep still water. Then as the summer goes on—that is to say, the end of the summer—the end of July and August—when both fish are in good condition, perhaps the only rule of guidance to be taken is that of the trout being under the banks and the grayling more frequently in the middle of the stream, excepting perhaps in the case of what our northern friends call *dubs,* which are long stretches of smooth water of any length, from twenty to two hundred yards, of moderately uniform depth of three to, say, five feet, and with a current pretty steady throughout. Now if in these dubs a good sprinkling of rises are to be seen, probably they will be grayling; and when a grayling does rise near the bank it may always be taken as an extra heavy one, and very likely an extra wary one, and it will rise at shorter intervals than a trout.

One particularly aggravating feature about both trout and grayling is the pertinacious way in which they will feed just at the time when they are out of season—that is to say, the number of grayling that one has to return in the spring, and the extraordinarily large ones too, and the number of trout, and very large trout too, taken in October and sometimes in November, are certainly most annoying; but still there is a consolation if one returns these large fish, and returns them with care—one may know pretty well if they are in the stream there is a chance of catching them another time. Perhaps this would not console some of our pot-hunting friends much.

Trout as a rule when feeding, and feeding steadily, keep very much in one spot. They do not as a rule travel far while feeding, and if they do they generally travel up-stream. Now a feeding grayling is in quite a different position. He ranges over a considerable area. He deviates from the right to the left, up and down, but seldom is a persistent traveller. The reasons for these peculiarities of rises are not difficult to find. It only requires a small amount of study of the fish and its habits to point out the reasons of it. A rising trout places himself near the surface of the water, so that to take in the fly floating down over him he has only to slightly raise his head and open his mouth. Hence he places himself in a position where a continuous stream of the particular form of fly he is feeding on is floating down, and if he should have a desire to shift his position, it will probably be up the particular run where he can see a continuous and apparently unending stream of food floating down towards him.

With the grayling the case is different. A grayling even when rising well is probably not less than two feet below the surface, and in some instances much lower down ; and to look at him anatomically, it really does not appear that he was ever intended to feed on surface foods at all, as the mouth of a grayling in a horizontal position seems to be more adapted for picking up an object from the bottom of the river than for feeding on the surface.

However, our grayling is, as before stated, at a depth of about two feet below the water, and out of those curious pear-shaped eyes of his he is carefully scanning every object floating over his head. Presently he sees within the limited area of his vision—and there is good reason to believe that the area of vision of all fish is somewhat limited—what looks to him like an insect of the sort he likes to feed on. He rises towards the surface, and if he has calculated his distance exactly he secures it. A very small miscalculation, however, in rising through

that depth of water will throw him out, and hence
the reason why the grayling so frequently rises falsely,
whether at the natural or at the artificial fly.   Having
taken or having missed his fly, he again retires to the
comparative depth at which he is lying, until attracted
by some other fresh passing insect.   Now a very
small amount of consideration will show that the
rays of light entering the eye of the grayling at the
lower depth will spring from a far larger area than
those entering the eye of the trout comparatively
near the surface, and the grayling will therefore see
flies covering a much wider area and be likely to
take them.   There is very often a kind of flash or
flick of the fin caused by the dorsal fin of a grayling
when rising, although the fin itself is not altogether
visible.   This particular kind of rise is eminently
characteristic of the grayling, and of comparatively
small or medium-sized ones, say from a pound to a
pound and a half, the larger ones affecting a slow
subdued rise, much more like that of the trout.

Although there are many places in which the
angler must be doubtful, when seeing the rise, as to
the probability of its being a trout or a grayling, there
is one place where he may be almost invariably
certain that it is a grayling, and this place is the
final portion of a smooth glide above a rough run,
just where the water is breaking, or in a similar
position at the very point where the smooth water
pours over a short fall, and in this latter case it seems
almost impossible that a fish could remain in such

a position. Yet grayling do, and sometimes rise well there; of course excepting when, in the very act of taking the fly, they are comparatively deep down in the water where there is no current. As may be expected, and as pointed out before, in this as in any other position they very often miss either the natural fly or the artificial. The faster it travels the more likely they are to miss it, and the advice can fairly be given that so long as it does not drag it is impossible for it to go too slowly; or, to borrow from the salmon-fishermen one of their phrases which admirably describes it, where possible it is well to *hang* the fly in such a position. Grayling certainly when rising do so more frequently than trout, and although they cannot be said to be less shy, they certainly are more tolerant of being fished for, and when only lying in position comparatively deep down in the water can sometimes by a pertinacious angler be worried into taking the fly.

There are many reasons why grayling should be introduced into trout streams, provided there is plenty of food for both, and from an angling point of view the strongest is, that it practically gives three extra months of fishing without doing the trout any particular harm. Both these fish are, as a rule, not at the same time in the same class of water. The grayling take to the stream when the trout are dropping out into the deeper water after spawning, and *vice versâ*. As to the destruction which each causes to the other, there are many points to be con-

R

sidered ; probably grayling eat the ova of the trout
in considerable numbers, but so do many other living
things which are tolerated by those who strictly
preserve rivers, notably some of the water-birds, such
as ducks and swans, not forgetting our so-called
harmless friend the dabchick ; and probably if these
birds were exterminated from thoroughly preserved
trout-streams we should hear less of the destruction
of ova wrought by the grayling.   On the other hand,
the trout not only eat the ova, but the young fry of
both their own species and that of the grayling,
while the grayling only feeds on the ova, and does
not, I believe, touch the trout alevins ; so that, after
all, perhaps the trout themselves are more destructive of their own species than the much-maligned
grayling.

There is one marked peculiarity of a grayling
when hooked, viz., that it seems to have a far more
wholesome dread of the net than trout, and it
not infrequently happens with large ones, that
when, to the fisherman's notion, they are apparently
tired out, the angler, holding his net in the water,
gives the grayling a view of it, and he seems to get
a sort of new lease of life.   Off he starts, with so
rapid and brilliant a rush as frequently to eclipse all
his former efforts.   This is certainly a very dangerous
position.   It seems so surprising that the fish, which
has been almost on its side, and apparently at the
mercy of the angler, should all of a sudden muster
courage and strength for so determined a prolonga-

tion of the struggle, and if the angler has to any degree lost his presence of mind at the suddenness of it a catastrophe is often imminent. Of course if, in his excitement, the fisherman should by chance have tightly gripped his line to the rod for the final *coup* with the landing-net, the effect will be disastrous—either a break, or the fish will come unhooked and wobble down-stream on the surface of the water, so done up that if the angler has a friend with him who can use a net, he can very often get the fish out of the water after he has come unhooked. This has happened to me with grayling twenty times at least in the course of my experience, and yet I can never recall to my memory a single instance of having succeeded in taking out with a net a trout who had once managed to get clear of the hook.

CHAPTER XIII.

THE MANAGEMENT OF A FISHERY.

FRANCIS FRANCIS, in his " Practical Management of Fisheries," says that in one of Sir J. Gibson-Maitland's ponds at Howietoun, where the trout are artificially fed, the trout, averaging 4 lbs. each, were distributed over the area in the proportion of one fish to each one and a half square yards in water five feet deep. I quote this sentence from the works of one of the keenest and most reliable observers as giving some idea of the extreme fish-bearing capacity of water under the most favourable but purely artificial circumstances. It would be at least most unlikely, if indeed not impossible, to achieve such results in any ordinary fishing stream; but it must be borne in mind that attention to the same points which produced so remarkable a head of fish in captivity may be applied with more or less success to any water suitable to the growth of trout or grayling, and once established, the head of fish may, without any great difficulty, be maintained from season to season.

Briefly, the points are—*Stock, feed, and protect,* and these constitute the pisciculturist's golden rule; and of these three heads I propose first to treat in

detail, followed by a few hints as to the management of the water, as regards cutting of weeds and
adapting the fishery to the natural wants of the
trout and grayling when established there.

Stocking may be effected in several ways.

1. By turning in large fish.

2. By catching fish in various tributaries or small
streams and turning them in.

3. By turning in artificially bred fry, yearling, or
two-year-old fish.

4. By either spawning artificially so as to obtain
the ova, or by purchasing eyed ova, and either breed-
ing them in hatching troughs, or, better still perhaps,
by laying them down in the stream on artificial redds
made in suitable places for the purpose of receiving
them.

The simplest form, if expense is no object, must be
to obtain and turn in adult fish of large size, say a half
to three-quarters of a pound, which may be caught the
same season, or left for a season or two to breed without fishing for them.   There are, however, in this case
two points requiring considerable attention—firstly,
to see that a due proportion of the fish turned in
are females, as in a state of nature it is doubtful
whether one male will fertilise the ova of more than
one female in a single season, and if the males are in
excess they fight and injure one another.   The second
point is, to pay great attention to the strain of fish
to be selected for this purpose, and introduce the stock
from rivers where they are known to grow to consider-

able size and are in the habit of subsisting largely on,
and hence rising freely at, the natural fly.   Probably
the best strain of all is to be obtained from High
Wycombe, as they combine to a remarkable degree
gameness, good flavour, size, and, above all, freedom
of rising.*   Next to High Wycombe probably Test
fish are to be preferred, and possibly there are
many other streams not so well known to the angler
from which fish good enough for all practical purposes can be obtained.

Of all others, however, the very best means of
stocking a fishery is to catch from any tributaries
or bye-streams what may fairly be called *wild fish*,
taking them from comparatively shallow streams,
where, from insufficiency of food, or depth of water,
or from there being a great quantity of fish, they
have no fair chance of attaining a large size.   Such
fish are naturally in the habit of shifting for themselves, whether as to picking up their food or keeping clear of their natural enemies, whether birds or
fishes.   The main objection to this plan is that it is
not generally possible to find sufficient naturally bred
fish in the streams for this purpose, and hence the
aid of the pisciculturist has after all to be sought to
supply the deficiency.   It must also be remembered
that the large trout as a rule head up to thin water in
the main or side streams to spawn, and after spawn-

* Mr. Andrews of Guildford, to whom I am indebted for many
valuable hints and suggestions for this chapter, says, "I consider Wey
and Tillingbourne quite equal to the Wycombe fish in all these points."

ing return to the heavy water, leaving the small
fish, when hatched, in the lesser streams, to die in
great quantities during hot summers, from extreme
lowness of the water or lack of food ; and of those
who survive these contingencies a vast proportion
fall a prey to the devastations of herons, kingfishers,
and other enemies ; so that, after all, it is an economy
of the stock to remove these young fry to the main
river.   A considerable number of them are left high
and dry in carriers running through water-meadows
when the hatches regulating the flow of water to
them are closed, and an intelligent keeper should,
where practicable, remove all the trout from these
carriers some days before the water-supply is to be
cut off.   If, however, the depth of water in a carrier
should be so great as to render the capture of the
fish impossible, they should be removed *immediately*
after the water has been turned out.   Hatch-holes
should also be looked over, and any large fish who
have worked up into them removed and turned into
the main stream.

As to the third method of stocking, viz., that of
turning in fry, yearling, or two-year-old fish, there
are many arguments to be adduced in favour of
either plan.   Fry are most inexpensive, easy to
carry, learn from the start to shift for themselves,
and more easily adapt themselves to the general
conditions than older fish.   Yearlings are far more
expensive than fry, but if they have been reared in
ponds or streams containing a plentiful supply of

natural food are certainly as a rule the most satisfactory, on the combined score of economy and efficiency. If, however, they have been artificially fed, a terrible percentage probably die from inability to find their own food. Two-year-old fish are very expensive, and it is at best doubtful whether they will breed for a season or two. Of course, however, they become takable fish a season sooner than yearling fish would under the same circumstances.

Of the fourth or last means of stocking, it is questionable whether in the present age it is worth while for any angler to take the trouble of himself spawning the fish and hatching the ova. Eyed ova can be purchased at a very small figure from dealers, who keep the female and male fish in separate ponds, and can thus obtain practically every egg from the female at the right period and fertilise them ; while to obtain female and male fish both at the requisite stage for successful fertilisation from the river is a matter of considerable difficulty, and in some seasons almost impossible. The eyed ova, when obtained, may either be hatched in troughs according to the instructions given by Mr. Andrews in the volume of the Badminton Library treating of " Salmon and Trout," or, as I hear has been latterly carried out with great success, by laying them down in suitable places in redds artificially made on the shallows exactly similar to those made by the fish, leaving them to hatch out and take their chance on the river. When, however, it is remembered how few out of a thousand ova ever arrive at the yearling stage, it will be seen that the number of eggs required to produce any satisfactory result must be very great.

The head of fish that any river will naturally carry must always be limited by the quantity of natural food in it, or, as Francis Francis pithily says in "The Practical Management of Fisheries," page 14: "The *value of your stream is in the ratio of the food it produces* and not an atom beyond." This food should consist of flies and their larvæ, chiefly Ephemeridæ, Perlidæ, Phryganidæ, Sialidæ, Diptera, &c., fresh-water shrimps (*Gammarus pulex*), cray-fish, various water-snails (*Limnææ*), &c., minnows, loach, bullheads, and other small fish, and of occasional worms, especially where drains or carriers run into the main river. Of these the most valuable are the different flies, shrimps, and snails.

The shrimp can without difficulty be introduced into any water suitable for it, and is what, in my opinion, gives the red colour to the flesh of a trout, but at the same time, from the fly-fisherman's point of view, is not so good as the insect food, as it certainly is not surface food, and where it is abundant the fish prefer it to the natural fly.

Minnows, loach, &c., are not, however, altogether beneficial to a trout stream, as they eat the same class of food as the trout, and before becoming themselves food for the trout will, beyond doubt, have consumed many times their own weight in provender, which should go, in the first instance, to the trout. Besides, trout who are in the habit of feeding on minnows and other small fry seldom rise well at the fly.

The artificial introduction of flies into rivers where they are not indigenous has been frequently attempted, the usual plan adopted having been to carry gravid females and turn them loose, with the intention of their depositing the eggs, and thus reproducing in due course the larvæ and the winged insects themselves. As far as I can gather, these experiments have one and all been unsuccessful; whether from the eggs not having been deposited, or from the conditions of the streams into which it has been sought to introduce them not being suitable, I have been unable to ascertain. The difficulties, however, of conveying mature insects any distance in perfect health are greater than is usually imagined. The confined space in which they are carried usually proves fatal to a great majority. A few may be carried as specimens, but it has never been successfully accomplished with large numbers.

On the other hand, the larvæ of some water-flies are comparatively hardy, and if not roughly handled in catching, and transferred under proper conditions, will mature and establish a stock. This has been conclusively proved during the past season. I have succeeded in taking and hatching the eggs of three different flies, two Ephemeridæ, the May-fly (*Ephemera danica*) and the sherry spinner (*Ephe-*

merella ignita), and one of the Phryganidæ, the grannom (*Brachycentrus subnubilus*). The larvæ, however, in every case died at a comparatively early age, due probably to the fact of their being kept in London water, comparatively stagnant, in a confined space, and very possibly without the food necessary for their subsistence. These experiments are now being continued under far more favourable conditions, and will, I trust, lead to the solution of this all-important question. Mr. Andrews, the well-known pisciculturist of Guildford, has been kind enough to undertake the arduous duty of super-intending and recording all matters connected with the hatching of these eggs and the subsequent rearing of the larvæ, and with the advantages of having at his command an unlimited supply of pure water and plenty of specially constructed hatching-troughs and tiny ponds, coupled with his great experience on all questions relating to this and similar subjects, there are, I think, very fair prospects of his ultimate success.

The next point to consider is that of protecting the fish from their numerous enemies. The most deadly foe of the trout and grayling is certainly the pike, who not only preys upon them from the very earliest stage of their existence until they have reached dimensions almost equal to those of their voracious enemy, who not only devours them in numbers which would appear incredible to any one who has not studied the subject, but who also by continual attacks renders

them so shy as to prevent their feeding, and retards
or even prevents altogether their getting into good
condition.   An unfortunate phase of this shyness,
from the fly-fisher's point of view, is, that in streams
where the trout and grayling are much hunted by
the pike they rise less and less during the hours
of daylight, from fear of showing themselves, until
at length the only possible sport is to be obtained by evening or even night fishing.   No sign
can be more certainly deemed conclusive of the
presence of pike in a stream than to find that with
good hatches of fly day after day the fish will not
rise, but only feed during the brief half-hour of
twilight or after dark.   No word used by the late
Francis Francis in condemnation of the short-sighted
policy adopted by proprietors of fisheries who have
neglected to keep down by all means in their power
this deadly scourge is an exaggeration, and yet in the
present day the same insane neglect of their own
interests is continued, while from all quarters the
difficulty and expense of leasing good fishing is ever
increasing.

To get rid of pike a continual war to the death
must be waged on them; no rest, no quarter must be
given; throughout the year, day and night, and by
every possible means they must be destroyed; and
one of the most important qualifications for a first-
rate keeper is the knowledge of these means of
destruction, and a capacity to put them in action.
The most efficient weapon in the hands of a man who

can use it is the wire, and wherever the pike can be seen, whether in ditches, carriers, or the main river, it can be used with fatal effect on all calm days and especially in hot bright weather. When the surface of the water is rippled by a stormy breeze it is, however, very difficult to make sure of a fish; and perhaps altogether it is a better policy not to attempt it, as after being scratched once or twice with the wire it soon gets too wary to let the keeper get near it. In very shallow water pike may be either shot or speared, and for the latter purpose the best spear is the *small grains*. The head of this spear is cruciform, with a barb at each corner, and a fifth in the centre at the intersection of the cross pieces.

Pike run up the ditches to spawn early in April, and this is manifestly the best time of the year to kill as many as possible, as preventing the hatching of a new generation. If a female and a male run up a ditch and the female is not very near spawning, it is a good plan to wire or spear the male and spare the female. In a few days another male will generally appear on the scene, and in this way as many as three or four males may be secured, as well as the female. This, however, is a dangerous experiment unless the greatest care is taken not to wait too long and let her deposit the ova. It is well, too, to note that the female is generally the larger fish of the two. In deep holes or backwaters, which cannot be reached by the wire, trimmers should be laid, and where there is little or no stream the forked form described in Francis Francis' "Practical Management of Fisheries," on page 44, should be used without sinker; but in deep water where there is any stream the same form of trimmer with sinker is preferable. There are also several forms of *cages* made for pike-catching. The best, perhaps, is one similar to the thief-net, but made of galvanised wire-netting. It is placed in the river or ditch and baited with two or three roach or dace. Sooner or later, the pike is tempted into the cage, and as it is made something after the shape of an eel-basket, when once in the trap egress is impossible.

It is advisable in every good trout-stream to net the water from top to bottom at least four times in the year—twice in the spring and twice in the autumn. It is a very good plan, too, to carry out each season's netting on consecutive days. The weeds should, if possible, be cut and the water drawn down low a few days before netting. Two trammel-nets are required; one—the stop-net—should be pitched in a shallow below deep water; the other net should be stretched across the stream three or four hundred yards above, and dragged down to the stop-net. Both nets should be drawn in simultaneously, one inside the semicircle formed by the other; the inner net is then landed first and the outer afterwards, thus securing any fish which may have escaped over or under the first net in drawing. The stop-net should then be carried down to a convenient spot, pitched, and the operation repeated. It is not a bad plan, for a change, to draw both nets down, one a hundred yards behind the other, as in this way many pike who have escaped the lower are caught in the upper net. If the water is clear and the bottom muddy a drag-chain drawn down in front of the net discolours the water and starts the pike out of the weeds and other hiding-places, besides giving timely warning of the position of snags, roots, or other obstacles which otherwise might entangle and tear the net. It is never safe to omit netting for a season, as jack who one year can pass through the mesh are large enough the next year to do incalculable damage. Besides, fresh fish are often attracted by food from adjacent waters, or are washed down by heavy floods. Pike seem to prefer trout to grayling, and hence the grayling fishing is often good in a stream after the trout fishing has been seriously damaged. Any coarse fish taken in the nets should be killed, as they compete keenly with the Salmonidæ for the natural food in the river, besides often wasting the angler's time and patience when rising at fly.

Large trout of, say, 5 lbs. or upwards, and especially long-headed lanky male fish, are quite as voracious and destructive as pike, and should be killed in every possible way, the more so as they very seldom rise to the fly, and when they do it is only at night.

The winged enemies of the fish must not be forgotten, and every available opportunity of destroying them should be taken by keepers or owners of

fisheries. The heron, who not only feeds upon the
adult fish, but from apparently mere wanton cruelty
kills and maims far more than he eats, and the
kingfisher, who preys upon the fry, and also the
smaller yearlings on the shallows, should be ruth-
lessly killed. Dabchicks, moorhens, coots, ducks,
and of course swans, who eat the spawn, should be
kept off the water.

Otters have a very bad name, and are considered
very destructive to a fishery; and no doubt in small
streams where there are no eels, pike, or other coarse
fish they will in a very short time nearly destroy
the head of fish in a well-stocked stream. If their
tracks be found, notice should be sent to the nearest
master of otter-hounds, or failing this resource they
must be trapped or shot. In large deep rivers, however, competent observers have assured me that they
prefer eels and pike to any Salmonidæ.

It is essentially the duty of the keeper to prevent
the ravages of poachers, and wherever a piece of
water is much poached, it may be laid down as an
axiom that he is at best inefficient or careless of
his master's interests, or worse, spends his time in
the village inn and besots himself with beer, or
worst of all, is in league with the thieves who are
in the habit of levying periodical toll on his master's
water. With an incompetent or dishonest keeper
nothing can be done to prevent poaching, so that
the only remedy is to discharge him and fill his
place with a better man.

Staking the shallows is advised as a preventive
to netting, but possibly it is not as useful as is
imagined.   Poachers as a rule pitch their net, a
silk trammel heavily leaded, at night, at the lower
end of the shallows, and drive the fish down to it.
If there are no weeds every fish runs to the net and
is secured ; and if there are weeds, those who take
shelter in them most likely escape.   Then, again,
the stakes have to be drawn before cutting weeds
if the chain-scythe is used, and poachers have been
known to take advantage of the intervening night
to drag the shallows, if they affect that style of
net.   In any case, no poacher would risk his costly
gear on any shallow without first making himself
acquainted with the position of any stake or other
impediment likely to damage his net.   Brick burrs
or old stone rick straddles placed here and there
on a shallow not only prevent netting, but also
make good hides and breaks such as large trout
specially affect.   Squares of galvanised wire netting about eighteen inches each way, rolled up with
the ends projecting, or old tin cuttings, are useful
for fouling and rolling up the nets; and broken
bottles are awkward things for the bare feet or
even boots of poachers, but are equally or more
destructive to the angler's waders.   Francis Francis
says that an old cart-wheel plentifully studded
with tenterhooks sunk in a deep hole is a capital
thing to stop the use of a casting-net.   *Drowners*,
as they are called in the south of England, or, in

s

other words, the men regulating the water in the
meadows, have exceptional opportunities of taking
the large fish out of carriers or small drains at
night or early morning. They run up these drains
to feed on worms, and a small landing-net is all
that is required to take them out.

Fish on a shallow require shelter for two reasons
—firstly, to enable them to rest when feeding out of
the main strength of the current; secondly, to give
them shelter within a moderate distance when scared.
These two objects may be effected to some extent
by judicious weed-cutting where there are weeds—a
subject of which I will treat farther on—and still
more by the use of artificial hides. These hides may
be made in several ways; brick burrs and straddles,
as stated above, may be scattered on the shallow, and
behind each of these in the slack water a fish will
take up its position. Often, too, a fish will be seen
immediately above the obstacle, in the wedge of dead
water caused by the division of the current, and such
a fish is invariably feeding. Weeds hung up on the
head of stakes break the force of the water, and thus
make hides under which fish will lie. The so-called
table hides are made by fastening a table or platform
of one-inch planks to four stout posts driven into the
bed of the stream within a foot or eighteen inches
of the bottom, or the table may be constructed and
afterwards sunk by loading with stones or concrete.
On waters where they are in use I am assured
that they make good shelters, and, strange to say,

when hooked fish very seldom run under them. It is scarcely necessary to point out that in establishing a fishery the order of procedure should be to kill down enemies and prepare water first, and then to adopt the plan selected for stocking the water.

Perhaps the most important question of all in connection with the management of a fishery is that of weed-cutting. If every scrap of vegetation in the shallows is shaved away the fish must be very shy, and when one is scared from the absence of shelter he rushes up or down stream for twenty yards or more, scaring on his way other fish, each of which in turn communicates the scare to others, until there is not a fish to be seen on the shallow. If, on the other hand, the stream is choked up with weeds, there may not be for some distance a single open place to throw to, and where there is an open patch a hooked fish has every chance of weeding and getting away.

Of the two it is safer to err on the side of too much rather than too little weed ; but, strange to say, there is scarcely a water in the south of England where the happy medium has been attained. The best method known to me is that called the *side and bar* system, the rule for which is, *side the deeps and bar the shallows.* To explain the meaning of this : throughout the deep water the weed should be cut along either bank for four or five yards, or as far as a man can reach with the long-handled weed-scythe. All the fish will then feed either on the edge of the weed, or more likely under the bank in the run of clear water. The chain-scythe should never be used excepting on mill ponds, and there in the interests of the miller rather than the angler. So far it is all plain sailing, but the management of the shallows requires far more judgment. To assist in showing the *bar system* I have taken from the Ordnance Map a portion of the well-known Sheepbridge shallow at Houghton, and shown on Plate XXV. how it would appear if thus treated. The plan consists in leaving alternate bars of weed and clean gravel each from ten to twenty yards wide. The gravel is cleaned by harrowing across the stream, and kept clean by an annual repetition of the treatment if necessary.

Any hides or burrs would probably be unnecessary with this treatment, as the fish would lie either under the shelter of the weeds or among them. The abundance of weeds left would ensure a sufficiency of insect and other food, and make it difficult for poachers to net the shallow. If netting is necessary in the interests of the fishery, weeds can be cut at the end of the season for the purpose. Should these bars of weed back the water up too much, as many longitudinal cuts as necessary can be made through the weeds, and the current can be diverted to any spot desired by making these longitudinal cuts leading towards such spot.

Much inconvenience is caused by cut weeds drifting down from other waters above; in fact, many of the best fishing days are frequently partially, if not entirely, spoilt by the owners of waters above either

PLATE XXV.

MANAGEMENT OF A FISHERY

Sheepbridge Shallow at Houghton.

Leighton Brothers. *Lith.*

D.Moul. del.

designedly or thoughtlessly sending down their weeds. It is very easy to obviate this by stretching across the upper part of a fishery at a narrow and not very rapid part a heavy large-meshed net, a couple or three feet deep, with the lower side weighted, attached to strong posts on either bank. The large masses of floating weeds gradually accumulate, and in time form a barrier, effectually preventing even the smallest pieces from passing through. At the end of the day's fishing, or at any time, if the strain becomes too great, the mass can be liberated by slacking away the rope attached to one end of the net, and replacing it when requisite. The weeds thus liberated drift down in a body, and will only interfere with the fishing for, say, a quarter of an hour, instead of spoiling the whole day.

It is desirable to make some definite rules as to the conditions under which fishing is to be carried on, more particularly as to the season during which fish may be killed, the limit of size, restrictions as to what baits may be used, and the season during which wading should be prohibited to prevent injury to spawning beds and young fish. Taking the Test as a type, the rules as appended meet with general approval, and may be varied to suit the conditions of other rivers. Season—Trout, April 15 to September 15. Grayling—July 1 to December 31. Bait—Artificial fly only. Size—Trout or grayling under twelve inches to be returned to the river. Wading not allowed between November 30 and

April 30.   *N.B.*—In May-fly waters the limit of
size during the May-fly season may, I think, be
advantageously raised to, say, fourteen inches, but
this must be regulated to the capacity of the particular stream.   I may add that, as regards undersized fish, where the stock is plentiful, an average
which results in the keeping of about one-third of
the fish caught is a fair thing for the stream if the
stock is to be kept up.   I have lately heard of a
plan adopted by the lessee of a celebrated fishing
on the Kennet, and commend this generous treatment of a stream to all anglers who have the ultimate
good of the river at heart.   During the last two
months of trout fishing, August and September, he
returns uninjured to the water every female fish
landed, and as experience shows that during these
months ten females are caught for every male, the
self-denial practised by this true sportsman is an
example which should be followed by all desirous
of deserving this noble title.   It is an established
fact that in a river which is heavily fished, when
netting at spawning-time the proportion of sexes
shows thirty males to every female, and I think
the plan of killing off some of them is extremely
judicious.

In conclusion, and before taking leave of my
readers, the following advice is tendered.   Before
taking a water see that it is adapted for trout or
trout and grayling ; that the water-supply does not
fail during the hot weather, and is as much as pos-

sible under your control; that there are shallows or tributaries for spawning, as well as deep water for large fish in hot weather. A reasonably long lease should be secured, unless the water is already well stocked, or you may find yourself in the disagreeable position of having expended a considerable sum in improvements, with the result of either having your rent raised in consequence of these very improvements, or worse still, finding the water let over your head to some other tenant, who will benefit by your expenditure, and very possibly impoverish the water during his tenure.

Finally, to all honest anglers a word of advice—Fish fair, never take undersized or ill-conditioned fish, never refuse to brother angler a day's fishing or a pattern fly, and give as freely and fully as I have endeavoured to do the benefit of any discovery you have made or experience you have gained in the great case of " Angler *v.* Fish."

INDEX.

A BAD light, 151.

Accuracy with under-handed cast, 56.

Action of a rod, 17.

Adult fish, stocking with, 261.

Advantages and disadvantages of grayling in trout-streams, 251, 257.

Advantages, comparative, of dry-fly and wet-fly, 37.

—— of casting up-stream, 64.

—— of double-handed rod, 2.

—— of selecting apparently unfavourable places, 78.

—— of single-handed rod, 2.

Air and water, temperature of, as affecting hatch of duns, 140.

Air-pump, use of, in dressing reel-lines, 23.

Angler's friend, 225.

April, selection of fly, 164.

Artificial fly, dragging caused by travelling too quickly, 83.

Artificial fly, dragging caused by travelling across natural set of stream, 88.

Artificial fly, dragging caused by travelling too slowly, 87.

Artificial May-fly, occasional use of, after May-fly season is over, 191.

Artificial May-flies, size of, 186.

Attaching eyed hooks to cast, Hall knot for, 30.

Attaching eyed hooks to cast, Turle knot for, 31.

August, selection of fly, 194.

Autopse, how to, 232, and Plate XXI.

Autopsy, floating portion of, 233.

Autopsy, sunk portion of, 237.

Autopsy, lessons to be learned from, 243.

Average number of eggs laid by May-fly, 174.

BAY, slow-running, fish rising in, 86, 106.

Beaufort scale, 155.

Bickerdyke point-ring, 14.

Blue-winged olive (*Ephemerella ignita*), 206.

Boiled oil for dressing reel-lines, 23.

Box for flies on eyed hooks, 32.

Brass reels, 20.

Bridge or hatch, fish rising just above, 80.

Bright sun, as influencing sport, 150.

Brogues, fastening, 34.

Bulging, definition of, 116.

Bulging fish, patterns for, 123.

Bulging, indications of, 121.

Butting a fish, 220.

CADDIS and cases (*Phryganidœ*), 238, and Plates XXII. and XXIV.

Cœnis lactea (Pictet), 203.

Cœnis rivulorum (Eaton), 203.

Captivity, eggs of Ephemeridæ hatched in, 266.

Captivity, eggs of Phryganidæ hatched in, 267.

Captivity, May-fly eggs hatched in, 174.

Carrying mackintosh, 34.

Celery beds, 91.

Cast, accuracy with under-handed, 56.

—— dry-fly switch, 63, and Plates XII. and XIII.

—— over-handed, 47, and Plates II., III., and IV.

—— steeple-, 61, and Plates IX., X., and XI.

Trout and grayling streams, otters in, 272.
—— and grayling streams, means of killing pike in, 268.
—— and grayling streams, pike in, 267.
—— diet of grayling more various than that of, 241.
—— for stocking, best strains of, 262.
—— in September, 195.
—— jumping, 118.
—— minnowing, 111.
—— playing a, hooked, among heavy banks of weeds, 225.
—— rising and travelling up-stream simultaneously, 114.
—— streams, advantages and disadvantages of grayling in, 251, 257.
—— streams, dace rising in, 93.
—— voracity of large male, 271.
—— when rising, to distinguish grayling from, 252.
—— when weeded, tactics to pursue, 224.
—— weeding, 223.
Turned-up eyes for hooks, 29.
Turle knot for attaching eyed hooks to cast, 31.
Turned-down eyes for hooks, 29.
Two-year-old fish for stocking, 264.
Tying strands of gut together, knot for, 28.
Typical fish to cast for, 73.

UNDER-HANDED cast, 53, and Plates VI., VII., and VIII.
—— accuracy with, 56.
—— difficulties of acquiring, 55.
—— positions where specially useful, 55.
Upright rod-rings, 14.
Up-stream casting, advantages of, 64.
Use of air-pump in dressing reel lines, 23.
Use of the chain scythe, 276.
Use of the landing-net, 229.

VARIETY of food found in fishes, stomachs, 242.
Varnish for rods, 11.
Various sorts of smuts, 133.
Various ways of stocking, 261.
Very shy fish (Ronald's), when to cast to, 106.
Voracity of large male trout, 271.

WADERS, 32.
Water and air, temperature of, as affecting hatch of duns, 140.
Weather, dry-fly in rough or rainy 43.
Weather as influencing sport, 138.
Weed-cutting on shallows, 275.
Weed-cutting, side and bar system of 275.
Weed-patches, tails of, 75.
Weeded, when trout, tactics to pursue, 224.
Weeding, trout, 223.
Weeds, cut, to prevent from drifting down, 276.
Weeds, heavy banks of, playing a trout hooked among, 225.
Weeger winch fittings, 15.
Wells, Henry P., on manufacture of split-cane rods, 8.
Wet box for gut, Mr. Hawksley's, 27.
Wet-fly and dry-fly, comparative advantages of, 37.
Wet-fly, circumstances favourable to, 39.
When to cast to grayling, 108.
When to cast to a very shy fish (Ronald's), 106.
When not to throw, 106.
Whipping greenheart rods, 11.
Whipping split-cane rods, 10.
Wild fish for stocking, 262.
Winch fittings, 15.
Winch fittings, Weeger, 15.
Winged enemies of fish, 271.
Willow flies in grayling, 249.

YEARLINGS for stocking, 263.